The Kids
Will Be Fine

The Kids Will Be Fine

Guilt-Free Motherhood
for Thoroughly Modern Women

Daisy Waugh

Metropolitan Books
Henry Holt and Company
New York

Metropolitan Books
Henry Holt and Company, LLC
Publishers since 1866
175 Fifth Avenue
New York, New York 10010
www.henryholt.com

Metropolitan Books® and m® are registered trademarks of
Henry Holt and Company, LLC.

Originally published in the United Kingdom in 2013 under the title
I Don't Know Why She Bothers by Weidenfeld & Nicolson, London.

Library of Congress Cataloging-in-Publication data

Waugh, Daisy.
  [I don't know why she bothers]
  The kids will be fine : guilt-free motherhood for thoroughly
modern women / Daisy Waugh.
        pages cm
  "Originally published in the United Kingdom in 2013 under the
title, I don't know why she bothers by Weidenfeld & Nicolson,
London"—Title page verso.
  Includes index.
  ISBN 978-1-62779-012-3 (hardback) — ISBN 978-1-62779-013-0
(electronic copy) 1. Motherhood. 2. Parenting. I. Title.
  HQ759.W36 2014
  306.874'3—dc23   2013042579

Henry Holt books are available for special promotions and premiums.
For details contact: Director, Special Markets.

First Edition 2014
Designed by Meryl Sussman Levavi
Printed in the United States of America

10 9 8 7 6 5 4 3 2 1

For my children, doing fine so far

Contents

Part III: Child Care

Because Easygoing Parenting Saves You Time
and Money and Is Good for the Whole Family

Part IV: School

Part V: Charm School

The Kids
Will Be Fine

Motherhood

Some Potentially Liberating Observations

Researchers have found that children born to older mothers have stronger language skills and face fewer social and emotional problems compared to children born to younger mothers.

Recent studies show that children of older mothers are more at risk for autism.

Studies have shown later development, poor verbal skills, and lower test scores of children whose mothers returned to work in the early months of their babies' lives.

Researchers have found that mothers who are overinvolved or overprotective during the early stages of a child's development can increase the risk for anxiety later in the child's life.

Recent studies have shown that babies who are breast-fed exclusively for the first six months of life are at greater risk for developing nut allergies.

Recent studies show that infants who are breast-fed are less likely to suffer ear infections.

*

It is tempting when trying to make a point (especially an argumentative one: namely, most of what follows) to do a quick foray through Google in search of a study or statistic to back it up. Look hard enough and there will almost certainly be one. And although studies per se are clearly a good thing when used to illustrate a strong point of view, they are probably best taken with a pinch of salt. The above selection of beguiling but contradictory information took me about half an hour to cobble together while waiting for my yoga class to begin.

There are lies, there are damn lies, and there is Google for some slick-sounding studies to back them up. I am going to resist the temptation to bamboozle us all with studies.

*

I was at a working lunch not so long ago, sitting at a big table, surrounded by clever, accomplished men. In a roomful of twenty or more, only four of us were women: an Estonian intern in her early twenties who didn't seem to speak any English; an expert of some kind, a gentle, unassuming woman; a secretary to the man hosting the lunch; and me, out of my depth, outnumbered, and a bit distracted. But the food was good, and it made a change from writing.

One of the guests was an expert on welfare reform. (This story gets better.) He was a highly respected gentleman with a mean mouth, I noticed, and a good suit; he was advising the current government, as he had the last, on sundry initiatives related to welfare-dependent single mothers. Maybe—

who knows?—some of his illiberal-sounding initiatives might indeed prove helpful one day, but in my heart I doubted it, if only because of the scorn-filled tone he used to discuss them. He had statistics aplenty and an unshakable confidence in his own rectitude, and also a noticeable dislike for the people he proclaimed himself so keen to help.

In any case, call it sentimental (I'm sure he would), but it seemed to me that, statistics or no statistics, any child-rearing initiatives devised by men with mean mouths and smart suits enjoying extravagant weekday luncheons in Mayfair dining rooms where there weren't enough women present were unlikely to bring much wisdom or kindness to the effort.

The main gist of the man's intended reform was faintly reminiscent of that creepy Tom Cruise film *Minority Report,* in which, thanks to a brilliant fortune-telling computer, government officers could incarcerate villains for "pre-crimes" before they'd had a chance to think of committing them. The mean-mouthed man wanted to send parental instruction officers—I'm not sure what name he had devised for them— into the homes of young, single mothers who looked as though they might yet prove unfit for the difficult task ahead. These girls, the men around me agreed, simply hadn't the faintest idea what was required of them, and they needed to be told.

Quite quickly, the conversation took what I felt was a nasty turn; if I'd known I was going to write about it later, I would have made notes. At the time, I sat as politely as I could while the steam began to whistle inside my ears. Mr. Thin Lips delivered his statistics and anecdotes with a sneering viciousness, and the clever men of Mayfair—of all political persuasions—nodded and sighed and rolled their eyes at the desperate state of the masses until the plates were cleared for dessert.

What these mothers needed . . . What these girls failed to appreciate . . . What these women had to be made to understand . . . Some of these little children, we were told, arrived at school having been so horribly neglected by their so-called mothers, they couldn't recognize their own names. They couldn't dress themselves. They weren't potty trained. They'd never laid eyes on a book. Many of them couldn't even speak properly. The single skill guaranteed to these children, it seemed, was the ability to open a large package of potato chips.

God knows there are some cruel and irresponsible mothers out there, and I've no doubt that in the course of his research, Thin Lips had encountered more than most. But something in the tone of these men, how lightly they dismissed these apparently hopeless women, how easily and complacently they judged and damned their maternal efforts, crystallized an irritation that had been bubbling away for years. I have to say that the anger I felt, listening to them sneering and despairing from their easy moral high ground, took me quite by surprise. You know how it is: one minute, you're sitting quietly, slightly intimidated, listening to the experts. The next minute, it occurs to you that some of these emperors at the table might, in fact, be naked. I looked at these men, from one to the next, and I wondered which of them had played what kind of a role in the potty training of their own wretched toddlers.

More to the point: What was the longest stretch of time spent by any one of these men, absolutely and entirely alone, with a child under two years old? A single morning? A weekend? Maybe even one whole, long, nightmarish week? Perhaps a wife had been in the hospital, the mother-in-law was dead, there were no sympathetic neighbors or sisters, no nannies available. . . . *But even then* (I thought), they would have known that such an arrangement was temporary. Some ghastly mismanagement on the part of someone else, probably female, had led them to this unavoidable situation. But it would be okay, because everyone would feel sorry for them and laugh indulgently at their incompetent efforts. And in any case, even a week of solitary potty training is bearable for a clever fellow in a suit, if he knows that, come Monday, he'll be safely back at his piss-and-puke-free desk, engaging his brain and, above all, feeling guilt-free leaving the potty training to somebody else.

Anyway, after several long minutes of listening quietly and smiling pleasantly at this VIP lunch, I started to feel so angry that my vision began to blur. "You go on as if these women were barely human!" I burst out, before I had quite noticed I was speaking. "But you don't seem to realize that the very fact that these chip-eating children still *exist* by school age is a testament . . ."—I didn't put it quite as neatly as this—". . . the mere fact that these children made it as far as elementary school at all is a testament to their mother's love. You're all sitting around sneering, but do you have the faintest idea how much effort and care is required simply to keep a baby alive?"

I said something along those lines, and I definitely said the bit about them sitting around sneering, thereby declaring war on the entire room. I rounded off my speech with a sweetener, a nugget of humor I thought might help smooth things over, while also, pretty much, summing up. "What I'm trying to say is . . . maybe a few rotten apples, like Stalin, for example . . . but on the whole, in general . . . I bet *the Russians love their children, too.*"

They looked angry and confused. "You're coming at the whole matter of motherhood from the wrong angle." (I tried again.) "You may not approve of what their children eat. But these women aren't raising children for your benefit and approval. They love their children. Even if you can't understand how or why."

To be clear, this book isn't about men. They are the least of our problems. I'm only setting them up as a common foe, so that the rest of us—the ones actually doing the potty training or feeling guilty about employing someone else to do it—can be loosely united, no matter what we feed our children, how hard we work or don't work, how too old or too young we may be. This is a book in defense of mothers everywhere who have had enough of the constant commentary—the stream of unsolicited, sentimental, impractical, and guilt-inducing advice on something that we might do far more enjoyably (and far better) left to our own instinctively irritable and lazy but loving devices.

Not all mothers love their children, of course. And I pity the infinitesimal few who can't, though not as much as I pity their offspring. But I don't speak for them, only for the rest of us: for that truly vast majority of women who, in our own imperfect and infinitely varied fashions, in the privacy of our heads and hearts, love our children fiercely and without the smallest shadow of doubt, yet who nevertheless sometimes feel the need to go to extravagant and impractical ends to prove it—not to ourselves, or to our children, but to an ever more censorious and sentimental outside world.

Modern parenting—like the men at lunch—disapproves of idiosyncrasy. It requires all of life to be laid flat and bite-size at the altar of a child's serenity. Leaving aside the spirit-sapping assumption that serenity is the be-all and the end-all of a well-lived life, it fails to take into account that loving mothers and their beloved children often want different things from the world, and from each other, too. We don't have to dance to an identical jig. In fact, if I may say so, we damn well don't have to jig at all.

And yet as the civilized world continues on its long and laudable trek toward greater tolerance in other forums, the Good Mother prototype seems to have got stuck—or worse, actually: it seems to have regressed, becoming ever more rigid and one-dimensional, to the point where even the smallest aberration from the simpering, slavish norm is scowled at. As any pregnant woman who dares to drink alcohol in a bar soon discovers. Such minor lapses in personal, prenatal care (if lapses they are at all) are now monstrous crimes: monstrous enough for total strangers to feel comfortably within their rights to approach and remonstrate.

We live, for the most part, in an unself-consciously selfish society. That's the way it is. It's how we've evolved and learned to survive. But future mothers are meant to set themselves apart: to forget everything we've been taught about the importance of "self-actualization," of "life being a journey," "fulfilling our potential," and so on—to cast all that aside and fix a hurried halo over our heads. Hopes and dreams, personal tastes and individual requirements—all the things that raise us above animals and make us human—become not simply irrelevant but faintly embarrassing. It's as if their mere existence might somehow undermine not only a mother's gratitude for the gift of giving life, but the magnificence of Mother Love itself.

What we have, for the most part, is repressive sentimentality, a smiling acceptance of female martyrdom that teeters, at times, beyond martyrdom into a sort of approved mass masochism. It's creepy. And it reaches its creepiest, most perverted climax in the delivery room, where women, for reasons that have never made any sense to me, are encouraged to endure the extraordinary pain of labor without calling on the perfectly safe and incredibly effective painkillers that we all know to be available.

I have three children. During labor for the first (before I knew any better), so pumped up was I, with nerves and hormones and fear of disapproval, that I allowed the midwife to negotiate me out of an epidural and into a hideous *birthing pool*. She said I was very lucky one had come free. So I lay in this idiotic tub, naked, frightened—and in agony—while my husband and the midwife stood awkwardly side by side looking down at me. Painful. Humiliating. Lonely.

But we learn. By baby number three I knew exactly what I wanted. And though the doctor rolled her eyes and looked queasy, and told me that "only the middle-class women" insisted on epidurals (perhaps because only the middle-class women are confident enough to demand them?), the hospital eventually relented. Better still—I had a husband who traveled, other children to care for, and I was living in a place far away from family and friends, so I had something called a "social induction." In other words, I was given drugs specifically so that the baby was born at a time to fit with my schedule. And—bless that scruffy little hospital—before anyone even gave me the induction drugs, they fitted me up with an epidural. Which meant, reader, a 100 percent pain-free delivery, at a time that suited me.

The midwife was an older woman: earthy, gossipy, and warm. We chatted up to the last minute about all sorts of things—her grandchildren and my children, *The Apprentice*.... At some point our conversation was interrupted by one of those shattering, agonized screams the likes of which you hear only on battlefields (I imagine) and on delivery wards where they're being stingy with the epidurals. The woman in the room next door, I was told, had "opted" for a "natural delivery." So natural, her screams made the flimsy walls between our two rooms shake. As the screams faded, and the poor woman paused for the panting exercises they no doubt told her would help with the next agonizing round of contractions, my midwife gave a merry, bosomy chuckle and shook her head.

"Another natural childbirth," she laughed. "I don't know why they bother." It's a question I've been asking myself ever since about so many of the aspects of modern motherhood that we're told to adhere to.

As I typed these words, I received an e-mail from a friend, written in hurry and rage, with a Web link to a precious-looking book called *Recipes from My Mother for My Daughter*. I will quote the e-mail verbatim: "For God's sake, look at it! Even the cover is so SANCTIMONIOUS! I'm pretty sure her mother never made anything with mascarpone anyway, because even garlic was barely even invented in the UK till the end of the bloody 70s!"

*

What are children for?

Depends who's asking, doesn't it: the CEO of Toys "R" Us, Sir Jimmy Savile, you, me, Joseph Kony, or the pope. Broadly speaking, I suppose, children aren't really "for" anything much, except for growing into adults so that they can have children of their own and perpetuate the human race. Which is nice.

But it doesn't really explain why, as individuals, we continue to go to the inconvenience of bringing our own children into the world. "Perpetuating the human race" was not even at the bottom of my list of reasons for having children. It didn't feature at all.

Bearing in mind what an appalling impact children have on our finances, sex lives, friendships, ambitions, our bodies, and our freedom—and bearing in mind the overwhelming sense of doom: the black cloud of world-at-an-endness that hovers between the Western consciousness and its broken ozone layer—and bearing in mind that the planet is already horribly overpopulated, that Venice is sinking, the ice caps are melting, the welfare state is unaffordable, the politicians are crooks, the world economic contraction is a Braxton Hicks to what lies ahead, that retirement's a pipe dream, and we're all going to die of cancer in a hospital corridor.

Bearing all this in mind, it seems extraordinary that we continue to breed at all.

Why? Why, above all, do Western women—with jobs and dreams, financial independence and reasonably full lives—why do we put ourselves through it?

Here is a list of possible motives.

- We are in love.
- We like the idea of being surrounded by a loving family.
- We want to feel needed.
- We like taking care of helpless creatures.
- Everyone else is doing it, and it's a bit lonely being the only one without a baby.
- Our job is boring and a new baby's a good excuse to resign.
- We've reached a stage in life where something has to change.
- It seems like the right time and we might regret not having had a baby in years to come.
- Our partner wants a baby and we want to make him happy.
- We're already pregnant and can't face having an abortion.
- To trap a partner who might be thinking of abandoning us.
- To take care of us in old age.
- It's a meal ticket.

- It satisfies a deep and primal desire to perpetuate, if not the human race, then at least our own stake in it.
- Because life is meaningless and, at bottom, we are all painfully lonely. And children, with the hope and joy they bring, help to keep our despair at bay.

No matter how you look at it, our reasons for bringing children into the world have nothing to do with the interest of a yet-to-be-born baby and everything to do with the interests of ourselves, or—which is the same thing—people we happen to care about. Mothers have babies—despite environmentalist assertions that the world would be better if we didn't—because, for one reason or another, it suits us. (A pregnant woman who refuses abortion, by the way, or who rejects lifesaving medication "for the sake of" her unborn child is acting according to her own moral code and for fear of her own eternal soul. She is no more selfless than the rest of us.) The point is, we are no less self-interested than the next man.

I find that rather liberating. We procreate not for the benefit of our children, not for the pleasure of friends, not for the approval of health visitors, schoolteachers, or thin-lipped government advisers, but for a myriad of expediencies, all of which lead to the benefit, pleasure, comfort, and approval—of ourselves. Mother love, as discussed, is a beautiful thing, bringing with it an abundance of collateral goodness: patience, kindness, tenderness—and, yes, self-sacrifice; but at the bottom of it all, motherhood is about us.

*

It was quite fashionable for a while, among the Mothers of America, to post the following message on their Facebook pages. It was a sort of Martyred Mom mission statement, from what I can make out, reminiscent of those stickers we used to tape onto each other's backs in the playground with "Kick Me" written on them:

> *To all the UNSELFISH MOMS out there who traded sleep for dark circles, salon haircuts for ponytails, long showers for quick showers, late nights for early mornings, designer bags for diaper bags & WOULDN'T CHANGE A THING. Lets [sic] see how many Moms can actually post this. Moms who DON'T CARE about what they gave up and instead LOVE what they got in return! Post this if you LOVE your LIFE as a mom ♥*

Barf bags disposed of? Good. Where do we begin?

It's absurd, clearly. And could be dismissed on grounds of breathtaking inanity. Nevertheless, in its clumsy way, it highlights what is a commonly held belief: that good motherhood requires a denial of personal pleasure and a negation of the self.

What's especially offensive about this particular manifestation, however, aside from the hectoring tone and the gratuitous misogyny ("Let's see how many Moms can actually post this"), is the implication, often made, though rarely so inelegantly, that "Unselfish Moms" should not simply rejoice in their children but should rejoice in all they have given up to be their mothers. As if the joy in the sacrifices (and what a driveling list they present us with: *salon haircuts for ponytails?*

Designer bags for diaper bags?) is a prerequisite of bona fide motherly love, and a mother who doesn't draw masochistic pleasure from such slavish self-denial is not properly fulfilling her role.

Yes, we know it. Motherhood comes with a million small costs, requires a million different compromises, and sometimes may even require taking a slightly shorter shower. But there is something a little sinister about the way the kick-me brigade harps on. And it makes me wonder, Why are they so aware of the costs in the first place? And—more to the point—*why oh why* must they insist on carrying on about them so?

In any other walk of life we laugh at them, the Pharisees, who make such a song about the giving and such a dance rejoicing at the cost. And we can't help but ask ourselves: What are they really after? What's in it for them?

Yet somehow the Martyred Mothers get away with it. Partly, I suppose, because for the fathers, at least, what price is a little sanctimony, if it means escaping from their share of the chores? And partly because the other mothers—who take on their motherly chores in a more brusque and businesslike fashion, and are often in search of shortcuts—tend to feel a little sheepish about their anti-zeitgeist behavior. I know I do. Or did. It's what drove me to write this book.

When the prevailing culture encourages mothers to confuse love for subjugation and when it endlessly reiterates and reinforces the same truth—that a mother who puts her own needs first is a bad mother and a freak of biological nature—it's tempting (though in our heads and hearts we know it can't make sense since we mothers never actually stopped being rational) to nod agreeably and say nothing, to smile obediently and shuffle quietly on.

Take, for example, the following concept: Me Time.

It's a ludicrous phrase and these days, to be fair, it's used as often in jest as in earnest. Nevertheless, the notion remains. And it reeks of a deodorized-panty-liner simpering-style femininity. Men don't talk about having "Me Time."

Me Time is the specialty of busy moms—moms who spend all day rushing around worrying, and who, every now and then, it is generally agreed, deserve a break from doing things for others: a few quiet minutes, after dropping off the kids at school, to sit down with a cup of coffee and a muffin, perhaps. Or, better yet, an afternoon in a health spa with the girls, discussing husbands and kids to the soft sounds of electronic lounge music.

I'm not saying there's anything wrong with any of that. I am only saying that implicit in the Me Time notion, no matter what form it takes, is the assumption that all non–Me Time is Other People's Time.

But of course it isn't. Yes, mothers spend much of their time tending to the requirements of their family. (Martyred Mothers far more time than they need to.) But then again, most adults spend much of their time tending to the requirements of others. It's called being an adult. It's called having a job. Mothers care for their children not because of some nature-given selflessness exclusive to them, but if anything because of the opposite. It's in a mother's interests to tend to her children because she cares massively—more than anyone else—about her children's welfare.

We look after what we care for. Me Time is all the time. It's called My Life, and it is always up to us how we decide to spend it.

*

The following sections are divided loosely into the chronological stages of motherhood. They are most adamantly not a guide. They are far from foolproof—in fact, they are not for fools at all. I don't aim to offer answers, rather to throw into the morass of blandness, sentimentality, and neurotic hyperactivity a few pragmatic suggestions and long overdue questions.

I only speak from my own experience as a modern, educated, middle-class woman who is more truculent than most (perhaps), especially when expected to jump through what may seem to others as harmless enough hoops. I don't think they are harmless. That's the point. They achieve nothing, they waste our living time, they encourage us to gloss our lives with bullshit. And the simpering demeans us.

There has never been a moment when I wasn't grateful to be a mother, but there have been many moments when I felt bewildered and alienated by society's inflexible expectations of me as a mother. And my sense of guilt at my failure to feel as blandly fulfilled as I knew I was meant to feel only intensified the sense of isolation.

So here are some potentially liberating observations for mothers and future mothers who might sometimes find themselves feeling the same way.

Part I

Pregnancy and Birth

And Some Pragmatic Suggestions

1. Baby on Board

I presume everyone (except for the people who put them up there) finds those "Baby on Board" bumper stickers irritating. Sentimental, self-important, and potentially even self-defeating, they assume that the driver coming up behind, on spotting said sticker and learning of Baby, is going to want to take extra care as a result. But why? With or without stickers, most people don't tend to want to drive into each other. The baby on board may be beloved of the car-sticker owner, but not especially to the stranger driving the car behind, who—we have to assume—will be doing his level best to avoid a collision in any case. He hardly requires an added disincentive.

Never mind. One of life's minor irritations, nothing more. But it makes one ponder the thought processes of the person who went to the bother of putting the sticker there in the first place.

Also, by the way: it's worth noting (since I may not be the only one on whom it has this effect) the sight of such a sticker on the back of a car often makes me want to crawl up its tailpipe, honking loudly. Only because I feel sorry for the baby, being landed with such disturbingly self-important and solipsistic parents and feel duty-bound to try to make the poor thing smile.

The "Baby on Board" badges sometimes seen on the coat lapels of pregnant commuters, on the other hand, serve a function. Worn in the hope that a fellow passenger might offer them a seat, they win their wearers my fullest sympathy and support. Also, actually, gratitude. How many times have you looked at a woman's swollen belly and exhausted face and wondered: Is she or isn't she? Should I be sitting while she is standing or is she just having a tired, fat day? With a "Baby on Board" badge, we all know where we are. Nobody fat gets unnecessarily offended, and nobody pregnant has to stand.

You don't spot the badges often. But the odd rare sighting makes me long to do more than simply offer my seat. I want to throw my arms around the badge owner and tell her, just in case she's forgotten, which she may have done because I often did, that pregnancy passes. Also—in case she's forgotten or doesn't know it yet—that the exquisite moment, at the end of it all, the moment it leads up to, when the baby is in your arms at last, out and about, and alive and kicking—that moment makes every long and lonely, mad and miserable month of its gestation worthwhile.

Obviously, I wouldn't actually do that. No. That would be irritating. Also—I should add—she might actually be quite happy, pregnant. Some women like it. I've heard them talking sometimes, on TV and radio.

But, my goodness—for the rest of us—for most of us, dare I suggest?—and with a million apologies to those women who are struggling to get pregnant, and with a million hidden parentheses regarding my own wonder and gratitude for having managed it at all—let's never pretend that being pregnant is fun. It is, on the whole, a drawn-out and fairly dismal experience. From the moment the first symptom kicks in, from the moment you tell the first person your happy news, and they grin at you and speak a little louder and a little more clearly, to tell you how you must be feeling: You must be thrilled!

Or no: from before that day, perhaps before you even suspect you're pregnant—when you begin, inexplicably, to feel a little out of sync, a little angry. And argumentative and hungry and inexplicably, ferociously bad-tempered.

Not everybody feels all of the above, all of the time. Even if they do, please understand I am not suggesting that the process isn't worth it. To win such an excellent prize is likely to command extreme levels of inconvenience and pain. Fair enough. Nevertheless, being pregnant is quite difficult enough. It's made more difficult—a far lonelier and madder journey—by the bland, conformist refusal to acknowledge what a peculiarly isolating and disconcerting process it actually is.

Baby on Board? You very probably do feel thrilled, among a million other emotions.

"How are you feeling?" people ask warmly. But it's rhetorical. Nice girls pull a little face. "Ooh, a teeny bit sick!" they say. Little face. "But really well otherwise!" I would rewrite those "Baby on Board" badges and hand them out, free, with every pregnancy testing kit ever sold. And they would read something like this:

"Sick, miserable, paralyzingly exhausted, frightened, lonely, incredibly emotional, horribly needy, fatter than usual, struggling with loss of my erotic capital, unable to drown sorrows in usual manner. But absolutely thrilled about the baby."

2. Being Public Property

Late on in one of the pregnancies I ventured into an unusually fancy cheese store, where a deferential middle-aged sales assistant, male, with a belly about the same size as mine, insisted on helping me make my cheese choices. I wished he hadn't, but that's what you get in fancy cheese stores. No peace.

Anyway, I ordered some Cheddar. Boring old Cheddar. Specifically because I could smell the man's bossiness above all the Pont l'Évêques and Camemberts, and I knew he was longing, perhaps more than he had longed to do anything in a very long time, to lecture me about the dangers of mixing pregnant women and soft cheeses, and I didn't want to get into the conversation. So I said:

"Could I please have some of that Cheddar?"

Over his own big fat belly, the man gazed at mine. I found him vaguely intrusive. I thought I'd buy the Cheddar and get the hell out of there, before he asked to feel the baby kick. He said: "Actually, madam, we really don't recommend it."

"Recommend what?" I asked. Snarled, possibly.

"I'm aware that doctors only tend to warn pregnant ladies about soft cheeses. But I prefer to play it safe. I personally don't recommend this particular Cheddar cheese to pregnant ladies. As I say to all my pregnant lady customers, it's better safe than sorry." He paused, looked unbearably smug, and, before I had time to clobber him, added: "Apologies if you think I'm fussing. But baby may thank you for it later."

He was trying to be kind, perhaps. It was harmless enough. Maybe he was just trying to break up the monotony of a long cheese-selling day. In any case, he could never have guessed quite how angry his comment would make me. Maybe if he had said it four months earlier, it would have simply dropped into the general swill of irritating and unsolicited pregnancy advice offered up by people who don't even know you. I might have been able to smile in a saintly manner and rise above it. But his comments, his infuriating assumption that I needed his advice, the insinuation that my unborn baby was in some way as much his responsibility as it was mine, came after eight months of the same: uninvited commentary, unwanted and unneeded instructions.

So I left the shop without the Cheddar. And blubbed with rage, all the way home.

3. Things to Avoid
When Pregnant

Hair dye

Hot baths

Soft cheeses

Cured hams

Shellfish

Heavy objects

Too much standing

Lying flat

Getting angry

Aromatherapy

Bicycling

Steam rooms

Being over thirty-five

Marijuana

Being fat

Being thin

Illegal drugs

Paint

Mackerel

Reaching up for things

Computer screens (CRTs)

Inhaling laundry detergent

Junk food

Running

Too much sitting

Vitamin A supplements

X-rays

Tennis

Tanning beds

Ticks

Lifting things

Microwaves

Aspirin

Tuna

Hot dogs

Reptiles

Sea bass

New mattresses

Lawn sprays

Salmon

Horseback riding

Dog shit

Soft-boiled eggs

Amusement park rides

Dog saliva

Contact sports

Flea collars

Red meat

Tap water

Paint thinner

Cleaning products

Electric blankets

Smoking

Pâté

Alcohol

Passive smoking

Bad thoughts

Salami

Coffee

High heels

Tea

Cat litter

Peanuts

The soles of your feet

Mayonnaise

Stress

Pop concerts

Water beds

The trouble is, of course, it's difficult to know, in the bottomless trough of impractical and officious precautions, what advice is worth attending to and what can be happily discarded. By baby number three I ignored pretty much all of it. Which isn't to say I went out of my way to breathe in pesticides. But I didn't go out of my way not to breathe them in, either. And sometimes—yep—after the initial morning sickness had passed (when even the thought of it made me want to be sick), *I smoked a cigarette.*

With baby number one, I wasn't so confident, of course. Added to which I was genuinely worried: the baby had not been planned and was conceived during a period of heavy-duty partying, in the course of which a quantity of unhealthful materials had been ingested.

I felt I had to talk to a doctor, just in case the damage I feared I had unknowingly wrought on my child might yet be rectified in some way. I was terrified. I envisaged the doctor inputting my sad confession into that giant computer, making an emergency call to Child Protective Services as soon as I left the hospital: I envisaged social workers with scales and rulers coming to my house, placing the baby on a watch list of infants born to unfit mothers, liable to be removed by the authorities at any time.

So I confided my worries, listing my poisons, with head hanging: "*. . . but you have to understand . . . it was before I realized I was . . .*" The doctor—bless her—burst out laughing. She was not your run-of-the-mill materno-sadist; rather, she was a kind and reasonable human being, and one to whom I am eternally grateful. "Never tell anyone I said so," she told me, "but as a rule of thumb, if it's the very early days, a fetus will either survive, no matter what you chuck at it—booze, drugs, and everything else—or it was going to die anyway. And if your baby has survived, as it obviously has—you have absolutely nothing to worry about. . . . Don't give it another thought."

I am not a doctor, and obviously I am not advocating binges of any kind—before, during, or after conception. Nor at any other time. In any case, it's none of my business. I am simply passing on something I was told by a doctor who was kind enough—and brave enough—to pass it on to me. Because it's something we have every right to know.

Fetus danger does not lurk at every corner. Which is why the world population has more than doubled in fifty years. Pregnancy would be a lot more relaxing if we could only be encouraged to remember that.

4. Shopping for Baby

It was always slightly depressing, in the old days, when friends and siblings started having their own families. You felt like you'd lost them to the Other Side. As indeed, in many ways, you had. When I confided to one close girlfriend, who at the time had no children of her own, that I, too, was abandoning her, she grinned dutifully, said, "Congratulations." And paused, to think of something else to add. "It's a fantastic new retail opportunity."

Quite funny. Or so I thought back then. But the joke wears thin pretty quickly, does it not? A fantastic retail opportunity it may be—for the retailers. An expectant mother (especially the first time around), all a-jitter with nerves and untried beliefs and goofy idealism, is nothing if not ripe for the fleece.

Wander the aisles of the dreaded baby chains, and the truth of this soon becomes clear. A truly craven new world opens up: a world that seems to be made only of germs and fear and sharp corners and worry, of bumping and burning, spilling, choking, and tripping hazards—none previously considered, and yet every one of which (it transpires) could be avoided with another piece of pastel-colored plastic and a few extra dollars. What price, after all, for your baby's health and safety?

It's been a few years since I needed to venture down those aisles. But I've just returned from examining the fare at one of those chains, and I see that—unsurprisingly—it has gotten worse. Was there, for example, a Miniland Thermo Advanced thermometer available ($81), with an "ultrafast: 1 second" reading, a clock with a "high/low temperature indicator" when I was last shopping for onesies? And if not, how did my babies survive without it? And had they invented that peculiar pacifier-like contraption, with the grisly gusset-netting sewn into one end, so that "baby" could suck on some food put inside it without danger of choking to death? I think not.

I'm finished with this stage of family life, and I am pleased to report that despite the lack of any chew-safe gusset arrangements, all three children emerged from their babyhood intact. This afternoon, with the baby-related terrors receded, I looked at the shelves of pastel crap being offered for sale to nervous mothers and snorted in disbelief. The cynicism, the fearmongering, the emotional blackmail, the bullshit, and the sheer fatuous, vacuous wastefulness of it all is truly breathtaking! How was I ever taken in?

Take the Doidy Cup—just for a small example. Sold in shades of baby-friendly colors at Britain's favorite shop (and no doubt elsewhere), it's a plastic cup with a "uniquely slanted" rim, designed, it explains on the pack, to encourage babies to drink from a rim rather than a spout, the "natural action" of which (what does that even mean?) "encourages good oral movements" (as opposed to bad oral movements). "Health professionals promote the DOIDY CUP," the fine print continues in its child-friendly scrawl, "to help prevent long-term health problems including: tooth decay, speech problems, poor chewing skills, poor feeding, anemia, failure to thrive."

Failure to thrive? It's a plastic cup with a slanted rim.

One afternoon, a month or so before our firstborn was due, the baby's father and I arranged to meet at a large branch of the spirit-sapping hell that is Mothercare, to stock up on whatever baby-soothing, hazard-avoiding equipment we might discover we needed.

It was—remember—the first baby. We were excited. We set out with quite a spring in our steps. But at the first, soft sound of the tinkly-winkly store music, something like stage fright—mixed with claustrophobia and horror—seemed to overcome us both. We didn't articulate it, so far as I remember. But this tinkly-winkly world was quite alien to our adult selves, as it must be to most adults, and it seemed to suck the oxygen from our lungs, the blood from our veins, the spirit from our very souls.

We must have spent an hour or two wandering those aisles, listening to that god-awful music, picking up "any-way-up cups" and "suction bowl trainer plates" and packs of nipple-shaped pacifiers, perfect for newborns. We emerged a lifetime later, the first dawn of awareness chilling our bones. This, then, was the world we would be inhabiting henceforth and from which (with luck) there would be no turning back.

We had spoken to no one in the shop and bought nothing except, in desperation, because I couldn't leave completely empty-handed, a small, cotton caterpillar with a bell in the tail. I left it on the bus on the journey home.

5. What Not to Buy

Thudguard

It's normal for young children to sustain bumps and bruises occasionally as part of exploring. However, learning to walk in a world of hard surfaces can turn a special moment into a heartrending incident in a flash. Consider for one moment being the height of an average toddler. If you're not sure about this, get down on your hands and knees and have a wander around. Look at all the furniture and hard surfaces you would hit if you fell—both inside your home and outside in your garden.

Now imagine you have wobbly legs, you're only just finding your balance, and you fall over more than you'd like to, because you're just learning to walk. Remember learning to ride a bicycle or learning to ice-skate for the first time?

What are the chances of you falling over and hitting something solid? Most homes today have hardwood floors or tiles, so statistically the chances are really high. The problem is that this kind of fall is very common in even the safest homes and gardens. The damage to a falling toddler's hands and knees can be an acceptable form of pain for learning, but a head injury can be traumatic for both infant and parent. Thudguard goes one step further and takes the protection straight to the infant's head, giving you great peace of mind.

According to the manufacturers of the Thudguard wear-anywhere "infant safety hat," "over 318,575 baby & toddler head injuries are recorded each year in the UK alone."

Fortunately, though, for $35.99 plus shipping and handling, Thudguard has come up with just the solution. The product is available in forty-five countries, and the company recently celebrated selling its millionth helmet. Top up on tranquilizers and breathe a sigh of relief, because thanks to the foresight of Thudguard, everything's going to be okay.

Of all the things that did actually exist when my children were babies that I was advised to buy but never needed—all the hideous pastel bits of overpriced plastic junk, the germ sprays, the noise-alert intercoms, the "nursing chairs" and changing units, the baby door stoppers and the "baby cupboard locks," the "baby aid" first-aid kits, the soft-glow safety night-lights—the thing I most resent having invested in is the electric breast pump. I resent it for reasons far beyond the money wasted. In fact, I resent it so much, it has its own separate entry in this book.

Aside from the breast pump (and the Thudguard), here, in ascending order, are ten of the most useless bits of baby-related junk currently available to waste your money on, most of which I myself have bought at some point and immediately regretted, and all of which, by baby number three, I survived very easily without.

10. Stair gates—an early warning statement to all newcomers that the adults in charge:

    a. don't understand their chief function as parents: to teach children as quickly and efficiently as possible how best to survive in an adult world. Toddlers who find themselves untended at the top of a stairway may well take a tumble. And, unless they're very stupid, will remember to take better care around tops of stairways in the future.

    b. don't know how to close doors behind themselves.

    c. lack any aesthetic sense.

    d. have officially ceded control of their environment.

    Proud to say—mostly because of the DIY required to install—our household never succumbed.

9. A diaper-changing unit. Thought I wanted this, first time around, but couldn't afford it. Used the bed, and weirdly it worked just fine.

8. An electric bottle warmer. Used a kettle. You should be aware that these can sometimes get a bit hot, especially if the water inside has been allowed to boil. As a rough guideline, if the water is bubbling (bubbles rising to the surface), it's very likely to be scorching hot. When handling a kettle (or any hot object), I generally advise mothers to arm themselves with a good pair of rubber-insulated oven gloves.

7. A diaper-disposal unit. It looked so high-tech in the shop. I had imagined, for the price, and with so many slick and groovy angles, that there would be some sort of garbage-truck, trash-crushing effect hidden within the mechanism.

But it turned out there wasn't any mechanism, hidden or otherwise. "Diaper-disposal units" are just trash cans—nothing more or less—with perfumed garbage bags inside that condense the stinking diapers into a point-less, gag-inducing, perfumed-garbage-bagged, stinking-diaper sausage chain . . . until such a time that no more perfumed packs can be squeezed within its slick lines, and the sausage chain has to be cut, the contraption emp-tied, and the aging crap hauled downstairs to an alterna-tive trash can. It's quite surprising, by the way, how much one tiny baby's piss and shit can weigh if you let it pile up in a sharp-looking disposal unit for long enough.

6. A Tiny Tatty Teddy Pregnancy Journal. I didn't buy this. Nor did anyone I know. Nor, in fact, did I even know such a thing existed until about two hours ago. I just spotted it for sale. It's pastel pink, and it has a picture of two teddy bears cuddling each other on the cover.

    Which is confusing, isn't it? Because the book isn't for Baby, it's for "Mom"—who, despite fulfilling a biological function only possible to a mature woman, is often assumed to have mysteriously regressed, as a result of her impending motherhood, into a teddy-cuddling infancy of her own. On the Tiny Tatty Teddy Pregnancy Journal sales blurb, it says:

Nothing can compare to the joy of becoming a parent! This Tiny Tatty Teddy journal will help you capture the memories made during the special time as you prepare yourself for your little bundle of joy. Your pregnancy journal will build into a precious keepsake, a permanent book of memories for you to cherish forever!

Being pregnant, as previously discussed, isn't usually fun. It's often ghastly. A process to be gotten through. A means to an end. I think we can do without the keepsake.

5. Any clothes made to fit newborn babies, most especially footies, unless you're willing to take scissors to the foot ends. Also, all baby clothes made of cashmere.

4. A Moses Basket. Costs about $80 and lasts for a maximum of three months, after which it's good for nothing at all. Too large for a beach bag. Too feeble to carry logs. Possibly good for a dried flower arrangement in the hallway, if there's room in the hallway among the rest of the baby clutter. Babies do look cute in them, no arguing with that. Then again, they tend to look cute anyway.

3. A baby bath. Another ugly piece of plastic, almost certainly pastel, probably embellished with teddy bears, and most unforgivably too bulky to store anywhere. Everlastingly annoying and truly pointless. What's wrong with the sink?

2. Room thermometers. For measuring the temperature of anything: rooms, baths. I've never understood the need for them.

1. A transformer-style stroller with baby carriage add-on. No matter with what high hopes the thing is acquired,

no matter how much it costs, how groovy its colors, how snazzy its snap-'n'-go, click-'n'-run, twist-'n'-shout attachments, the sight of the thing will be depressing within a month: rain-drenched, mud-spattered, with strangers' chewing gum stuck to the wheels and draped in plastic baubles, it'll be blocking the hallway. The bigger it is, the more expensive it will be and the higher the chance of householders stubbing their toes as they squeeze by. And the more elaborate it is, the more of it there is to snap and store, the more truly hateful the contraption will become.

I used a secondhand fold-up stroller with a seat that partially reclined. The experts tell you small babies mustn't use them because they need to lie flat, so I put a pillow in it, to flatten it. The end.

Total cost saved: impossible to say. Depends how crazy I might have gone with the snap-'n'-go baby carriage. Not far off a thousand bucks? Probably more.

6. Bonding with Your Bump

There's many a slip between cup and lip.... Or there isn't, actually, beyond a certain point in the pregnancy. But even so, it's hard not to be a tiny bit superstitious.... Bonding with an unborn child feels like a risky sort of a game, one that's quite hard to avoid, mind you, in the later stages, when even the baby's limbs are discernible. Nevertheless—for fear of tempting fate, I tried quite hard to fight it, against expert advice.

In any case, I don't think anyone really plays classical music to their bellies, do they? Or thinks beautiful thoughts for their unborn child's future peace of mind. It's just another thing-to-do or *not*-to-do, and feel vaguely inept for not attempting. All I do know is that of the three babies I brought into the world, the most easygoing, laid-back, and cheerful was the one I carried when I was on the point of divorce. No beautiful thoughts. No classical music. More vicious fighting than during the rest of my life put together. Stuff that up your peace pipe, baby gurus. Studies show (or at any rate, mine do) that a bump is a bump, however beloved. And it cannot read your thoughts.

7. Dads in Prenatal Classes

I didn't attend many prenatal classes, for lots of reasons. Because I was busy doing other things. Because I thought—as far as the actual birth was concerned—I wanted to think about it as little as possible until the moment it was upon me. But mostly because there seemed to be an infuriating assumption, during these classes, that we were all the same and ought therefore to be thinking and feeling the same way about the process ahead.

But I went to a handful, until the class when we were due to sit in a happy circle and watch a baby's head emerging into the world on a big fat cinema screen above us. It's bad enough, you know, watching a live birth, aged thirteen, in a biology lesson at school, when it all seems reasonably abstract, but to watch it with a round belly of your own, and in the company of a lot of men, was more than I could manage.

The biological realities of birth—in case no one's noticed—are not terribly beautiful. They are a grisly and painful means to a beautiful end. Also—I know it's old-fashioned—they're private. I don't want to discuss mucus plugs with anyone, actually, unless I absolutely have to. But I really don't want to discuss them with a roomful of unknown men, dads or otherwise. For men and women to remain reasonably alluring to one another—which must be an aim of sorts, mustn't it?—some details of our biological selves are better left unshared.

8. Fathers at the Birth

When our third came into the world, her father was sitting on a plastic chair in a corridor outside, almost certainly with a BlackBerry in his hand and, so the midwife reported back, laughing her bosomy laugh, out for the count: fast asleep. It was fine with me. To be brutal: he wasn't needed. Close by, for sure, but not in the room. As long as there were no complications, the birthing process was something I preferred to get through with as few people witnessing it as possible.

Each to their own. I know a woman who, along with her husband, her best friend, and her mother, also insisted on her *father* being present at the birth. It's a far cry from anything I would have wanted. But there you have it: we are all made in different ways. I find the current fervor for including the man in each and every stage of a process that, after all, is inescapably female, and in which he has no essential role, contrary, to say the least. And a little tactless.

After our second baby was born, the midwife asked if its father wanted to cut the umbilical cord.

"Probably not," I giggled.

The midwife sent me a malevolent look—and after all we'd been through together!

"I wasn't asking you," she said primly, pushing her grisly tools toward him. "I was asking Hubby."

He said: "Well, not really, no. But thanks."

A disapproving silence fell while she snipped away. And through our euphoria, Hubby and Mom were both struck with a vague sense of having failed their first test as the baby's parents.

We are not all the same. There is not only one way for a father to celebrate his child's arrival in the world. And though it may be fashionable for men to park themselves "at the business end" (and if there is a more coy expression in the English language, I have yet to hear it) during the birth of their children—scissors and barbecue tools aloft for afterbirth severance—it doesn't mean it's necessarily what they, or the baby's mother, would most prefer. Fashionable it may be; that doesn't mean it's best.

And, by the way, how can anyone seriously be expected to attach sentimental value to an afterbirth? Never mind the whole frying-it-with-garlic phenomenon (which I think we can all agree is cannibalistic and therefore a bit perverted); it's like attaching sentimental value to a turd. By the time either cord or afterbirth sees the light of day, it is human waste, nothing more—added to which, it looks completely disgusting.

Pity the men, though, in the birthing room. Neither nurse nor patient, just something tactful and slightly pointless, trying not to feel queasy. It must be difficult for them sometimes to know what to do with themselves.

But should a daddy-to-be find himself in need of expert advice, there's no shortage of places to look. Here are the highlights from a ten-point "perfect birth partner" checklist:

- Be aware of what she wants.

  If she has a birth plan, make sure you bring it with you to the hospital!

- Be a one-person support team.

  Do whatever she needs, from running to the cafeteria for a packet of candy to getting her another drink.

- Be prepared for surprises.

  "I ended up rubbing my wife's foot all the way through labor," says Chris.

- Look after yourself!

  The mom-to-be is the center of attention, but you'll probably be spending the night at the hospital, too, so don't forget to pack some things for yourself. . . . Pack a clean T-shirt. . . . Being able to change will help you feel fresher if you're up all night. . . . Comfortable shoes are essential.

Spare parts in soft-soled shoes. Poor buggers. And no flowers afterward. You've got to feel a tiny bit sorry for them.

9. Writing a Birth Plan

This always struck me as a harmless waste of time: a phony but well-intended system for lulling expectant mothers into imagining they have some kind of control over the process ahead. But I've since come to ask myself whether these plans may—unwittingly or otherwise—play a slightly more sinister role.

Consider this "Conspiracy Theory A": it's possible that birth plans are not, simply, pointless exercises for nervous, pregnant women, but part of a clever ruse. The reigning experts, as we know, try their level best to withhold epidurals from laboring mothers, no matter the searing agonies of the birthing process.

Imagine if, in a moment of weakness, you wrote in your birth plan, along with the usual optimistic requests for scented candles and hypnobirthing soundtrack CDs, that you wanted a natural birth, without painkillers—which, by the way, you're very likely to write (if you're bothering to write a birth plan at all) because it's what we are all encouraged to write, and it sounds good and healthy and maternal, and because, above all, it's impossible to imagine the pain of childbirth until you're in the throes of it.

But then the moment comes, and lo!, along with it the realization (as it does for so many women) that the natural option wasn't such a bright idea after all. You call for an epidural.

Your midwife might just hold up that idiotic bit of paper, written in a cozy living room months ago, when the threat of doctorly disapproval loomed far larger than the realities of such intense physical pain.

"Are you quite certain?" the midwife will ask you kindly, as you begin to scream. "Are you sure you can't hold out a little longer? We're doing so well. And we're so nearly there." By the time you have persuaded them that yes, you bloody well are certain, and no, you cannot hold out a little longer, and they have promised you for the hundredth time that an "anesthesiologist is on the way," it will be too late.

There tends to be a lot of pressure to go for a natural birth or a water birth or a birth with minimal intervention, and all sorts of reasons are offered, none of which make any more sense to me than the Silent Birth option, beloved of Scientologists.

The point is, if a woman could actually imagine—or fully remember—the extraordinary drama and intense pain of childbirth, it might be worth her while writing down a plan to cope with it all. But since we don't, thankfully, it's simply another time-wasting mini-task for mothers-to-be that, at best, teeters on patronizing.

I never wrote a birth plan. Partly because I was too

disorganized. For baby number one, I certainly meant to; but I think, even then, I could sense it was likely to be a fruitless exercise. If I were to make one today, this is what I would write:

Epidural, please.
Nice cup of tea with two sugars.
Thank you.

10. Don't Call Me Mom

It happens when the first nurse approaches the hospital bedside. "Mom" may be too bamboozled by her early landing in Momland to think too much about it, beyond a vague observation that the nurse is a little rude.

The nurse may not even bother to glance at Mom. She may only have eyes for Mom's baby.

"Mom," she will say, "do you want to pop Baby on the bed for me, so I can take a quick look at him?"

A.k.a. Mom, who stands before her, has a name. It shouldn't matter. A tiny scene, involving one careless nurse, a little too quick to patronize. Except, you have to ask: What just happened?

It was to be the first of many, many times I would be addressed by a fellow adult not as an individual but as a biological relationship. Even now, after all these years, each time it happens, it takes me aback.

There are only three people in the world who can call me Mom, and they know who they are. To anyone else: call me ugly, for all I care. Call me anything at all. Just don't call me Mom. I am not your mom. If I were, you'd have better manners.

Part II

Baby Care

And Some Possible Shortcuts

1. Bonding

Businesspeople, politicians, sociologists—they all invent words and procedures to lend their banal contributions to the national conversation an air of expertise. So it is with the process the baby experts call "bonding." Nevertheless, we must push through. You can't write a book about mothers and babies without talking about BONDING.

First of all: What is it exactly? I'm pretty certain it's what old-fashioned people call "mother love." This love, of course, in real life, just sort of *happens* (for the vast majority of us) and does not preclude feelings of irritation, claustrophobia, or really quite acute boredom.

But that's too simple for the baby-advising brigade; it renders them and their patronizing, faux-reassuring advice all but redundant. On the contrary, according to the website Kids Health.org (and a million others like it), "bonding is a complex, personal experience that takes time. There's no magic formula and it can't be forced."

Thank you, choir.

New mothers are reassured that most of the ordinary

tasks involved in the care of their new babies (*especially* breast-feeding, need I bother to mention?) are excellent "tools" for "bonding." Which is a bit like saying lungs are an excellent tool for breathing. Nobody's arguing with it. But unless the lungs are, by some unfortunate accident, deficient—in which case, ask your doctor for a referral—they don't need to be specifically and carefully introduced to a room full of air to know how to suck it in.

Needless to say, there is a font of advice out there on explaining to mothers how best to breathe. I mean bond. Much of which seems to end with the faintly cute injunction not to worry. But why would a mother worry, unless it's been suggested to her that the process of loving her own adorable but sometimes irksome baby "correctly" is in fact far more complicated than she realizes: that it requires books, articles, and uncountable websites to know how to do it properly, and that somehow or other she is almost certainly messing it up? "Bonding," we're told at MedicineNet.com, "is a big and sometimes scary word for new parents."

Aww, *come on!*

Askamum.co.uk says bonding with baby is "so important," they have provided a checklist of twenty ways to do it correctly, among them: "blowing raspberries on a tiny tummy," "regular morning snuggles under the duvet," and "taking a babymoon"—which suggestion, frankly, is so inane I refuse to translate it for anyone. . . . Okay, I will. It means, er—spending time with the baby.

The advice—and there is no shortage of it—seems to brook no middle ground. There is only one place to be when you're a loving and coping mother. (Luckily, with the right checklist anyone can get there!) And that is in the cloying, orgasmic land of Total Mommy Heaven.

"Begin by cradling your baby and gently stroking him or her in different patterns," advises ivillage.co.uk. "Smile" (baby centre.co.uk). "Look deep into your baby's eyes and watch how she stares back" (babyzone.com). . . . "Lie him on the floor between your legs and just watch. You'll appreciate what an amazing thing you've created" (askamum.co.uk). "Smell your baby and let your baby smell you" (ivillage.co .uk). . . . "Take a baby massage and/or baby yoga course" (bondingwithbaby.co.uk). . . . "Play peekaboo" (emmasdiary .co.uk). Only *do* remember, "if you hide behind a cushion, you must appear again, preferably smiling."

Now, I did say I wouldn't patronize readers with meaningless studies. But I wanted to share this little peach, brought to us, in all its negativity and uselessness, by the energy company E.ON:

> *Babies who are bathed by their fathers at least three times a week are significantly less likely to experience difficulties making and keeping friends later on.*

Anxiety isn't only a mother's problem. Or it won't be for much longer. Looks like the experts are coming after Daddy, too.

2. Breast Beating

Years ago I went on a long road trip with a small group of friends. Our team leader (who owned the car) was an astonishingly lazy man with quite a bad drug problem—not that it's relevant. I dislike sitting in cars. But some people really love it. The lazy man with the drug problem was one such.

We drove for eight hours across the flat American landscape (with pit stops for him and his habit) until finally we reached our hotel. The trip brought with it a useful epiphany about the myriad ways we each devise to satisfy our own particular forms of laziness. Some people love long car journeys. It allows them to feel like they are *doing something,* even though they're not really. That is to say, they are not doing anything that requires more than the bare minimum of movement and thought, but they're doing just enough to prevent them from feeling they ought to be doing something else.

I think, for many, breast-feeding offers the same sort of relief. Fair enough. And why not? Having babies, let alone taking care of them, is exhausting. And breast-feeding represents an excellent reason to sit very still for ages—and I do mean, *ages*—without anyone judging you for it: least of all yourself.

And that's okay.

Or it's not okay.

What do I care? Who am I to say? Sit or don't sit; breast-feed or don't breast-feed. I've done both. The sitting option can be remarkably relaxing and very cozy. But after a while—guess what? *It gets boring*.

Life is short. There is much to see and do. Spend too long on the sofa with your breast hanging out, drinking sugary tea and telling yourself breast-feeding aids weight loss (yeah, right), and the following things might happen.

Erm.

Well, nothing.

And for a lot of women (not all), "nothing" is not quite enough. Not when there's a perfectly decent alternative.

There's a new study every week, or so it seems. Non-breast-fed children tend to be less good at javelin throwing; more inclined to adulterous thoughts in their sixth decade; less likely to be good at reading three-dimensional maps upside down. There are studies, damn studies. And above all, before everything sacred, statistics advocating the superiority of breast milk. But the fact is, babies thrive on bottled milk— and the evidence for this is so bountiful, it seems faintly idi- otic even to have to point it out. Nevertheless—given the virulence of the pro-breast-feeding brigade, the patronizing bad-mother mini-puckers that the non-breast-feeders are confronted with day in and day out—I'll say it once, just to be clear: bottle-fed babies tend to get fatter faster, which I think we all agree is a good thing. They get fuller faster, thereby freeing up time for their chief feeder to be more than a human milk machine. Also a good thing. Bottle-fed babies stay full longer and therefore tend to sleep longer. Bloody marvelous. Everybody's happier. And yet, mysteriously, the experts frown.

So frown back.

3. Breast Pump

Ah yes.

Don't even take it out of the box.

And by the way, if anyone's ever wondered why women find it quite hard to feel like sexual beings again after childbirth, look no further than this odious little contraption. I bought one for the first baby; used it, I think, three times before chucking it in the trash. It's ugly, mildly uncomfortable, and, above all, it makes you look and feel completely ridiculous. Whoever invented it must have been a misogynist, sadist, weirdo, and pervert.

Or perhaps just a nice, well-meaning cokehead. The only person I ever found with anything to say in the contraption's favor tells me that her breast pump was invaluable after all-night drink-'n'-drug benders. The following day she would take care to express the milk that might contain residues of the previous night's excesses and throw it away, and then continue to breast-feed as normal the day after.

Pop, chop, pump, and hurl, she called it. And by the way, her children, weaned long since, are clever and kind, healthy and beautiful.

4. Babies at Night

Can be a nuisance. Mothers of newborns sometimes find it hard to think or speak about anything else. Which, let's face it, is often a good reason to avoid them. Poor things.

> *I generally put him down at seven p.m., but then at ten he tends to have a full diaper, so I try to wake him and sort of squeeze in another feed and then hope against hope. He slept through till four last Friday—which was fabulous . . . but normally he begins to whimper around three. . . . If I'm lucky, I can get him back to sleep again and he'll go through to six. . . . I'm trying to get him into a routine but . . . I hear him sobbing his little eyes out and I can't just leave him. I try—but by then I'm wide-awake anyway, and it just seems stupid: he's wailing. I'm awake. . . . And I'm finished. I don't think I've ever been so exhausted.*

Vast fortunes have been made advising women on what to do and what not to do to get babies to sleep through the night. Every baby expert has a theory—it's something they often seem to feel very, very strongly about—often promoting polar opposite opinions and techniques. And, I dare say, all the techniques work eventually, since humans, past baby-dom, generally tend to sleep during the night.

The one thing that all the experts seem to agree on, however, is that it's a rotten idea to do the one thing that actually works, and that most mothers instinctively long to do: namely, to plunk the baby in bed beside you and let it suckle. The baby goes quiet. Both parties conk out again at once. And it's lovely, actually. Better than lovely—really quite close to orgasmic perfection: peaceful, friendly, private, cozy, and loving.

Experts talk of crib death and our hearts stop still. They talk about mothers rolling over on top of their babies and accidentally suffocating them, but—unless a mother is truly, madly, and excessively inebriated and perhaps grotesquely fat—we all know in our hearts that it could never happen. For the same reason we don't roll over and fall out of bed every night. Only more so. And for the same reason that mothers wake up at the first sound of their baby's whimper (while a father can sleep obliviously through—or at least pretend to). There is an instinct to protect our babies that runs far deeper than mere sleep, and makes nonsense of the gurus' counter-intuitive and stubbornly joyless precautions. Defy them if you dare.

5. Leaving Babies to Cry

People have amazingly strong opinions on this one, too. Especially the older generation, whose "leave them to cry" approach (and I shall return to the matter of where to put disposable diapers shortly; it's the other thing that sends them crazy with irritation) sometimes, I think, carries a little hint of sadism.

"Babies cry. They need to learn. [*Learn what, exactly? I always wondered.*] If you keep picking them up, they'll never learn. . . . *We* were left to cry. It didn't do us any harm." There's no proof of that, of course. We might all have turned out completely different and much better if we'd never been left to cry. Too bad, too late.

The point is, there are systems—inflexible and diametrically opposed—whose proponents, as with the sleep training, are equally adamant about their rightness. Among the most noisome, currently, are Claire Verity of "no eye contact at bedtime" fame, keen on leaving babies to cry indefinitely, and Gina Ford of "Contented Baby" fame, keen on "controlled crying" (as if "controlled" crying were any different than "crying." Both involve leaving a baby to cry. But put "controlled" in front, and it lends the lack of action the sort of selfless respectability that guilt-ridden modern mothers so crave). And of course there is "Dr. Bill," famous for his unfeasibly inconvenient "baby-wearing attachment theory."

None of the three, I can't help mentioning, has borne babies of their own.

In any case, they're all bonkers, frankly. *In my opinion.* (Can I say that without getting sued?) Sometimes it's horrible leaving your baby to cry. Sometimes it's horrible not to.

No matter in what state of "horrible" we find ourselves, the sound of our own baby crying is, to most mothers, a specific and acute form of torture. My only piece of advice is this: when a mother finds herself in the latter state of "horrible"—i.e., simply cannot bear to be in the same room with the baby a moment longer—be sure to close any doors between you. Put yourself out of earshot. Switch off the baby monitor—and if its lights continue to flash, throw the damn thing in the trash. Give it to some other mother to torment herself with. You probably never should have bought the stupid machine in the first place.

6. Disposable Diapers

Herewith: a salute for the women who recycle their cloth diapers, who painstakingly pack them up into reusable buckets and send them off in vans to be sterilized—or whatever it is they do. Their saintliness leaves me reeling.

Everybody knows disposable diapers are not environmentally friendly. Then again, nor is having a baby. Nor is anything, really, when you get down to it. There are things I will do for the planet. And things that, since I'm bloody well living on it, I feel the planet must do for me. Finding a home for my offspring's dirty diapers has always fit into the second category. That's all I have to say about that.

The in-my-day, *never-harmed-me*, leave-them-to-cry, yellow-toothed-battle-ax brigade tends to get quite uppity about disposable diapers. They complain about the way young mothers put diapers in among household garbage (although disposable diapers tend to be wrapped in something often far more hygienic and less stinky than other things chucked into the household trash). Clever battle-axes strengthen their anti-disposable arguments by focusing their ire on the environmental impact.

But we all know it's jealousy really.

Never mind the pill. Never mind power steering, equal pay, maternity leave. Never mind the Internet! The greatest leap forward in modern times—for mothers, at least—has to be the Disposable Diaper.

I salute the Cloth Diaper Angels. I suppose. But in some bemusement. Life is quite chore-laden enough for mothers of diaper-aged children. I would suggest that such time-consuming and inconvenient attempts at saving the planet might be left for a less fraught stage in a mother's own life, and achieved via a less repellent method.

7. Feeding Baby

It all begins with the Lactation Nazis, as my friend from the Big Apple calls them: the kindly health advisers who tell us there is only one right way to feed our babies, and that everything else, though it does the job, will only ever be second best. Since just a tiny minority of women manage to stick with the recommended 100 percent breast-feeding approach for very long, most mothers launch themselves into the maze of toddler and child feeding with a now-quite-familiar sense of guilt and failure hanging over them.

I seem to remember that the dogma regarding when to start feeding a baby solids changed between one and another of my babies: from this to that, or that to this. God knows what they're advising mothers this week, but we can be sure that they'll be delivering it with the same dogmatic certainty they delivered the other advice the week before.

In the meantime, it seems to be reasonably obvious that you start feeding a baby solids when she's drunk all her milk and still appears to be hungry. But anyway . . .

A word on cooking for Baby.

The Beaba Babycook Duo Steamer-Blender, available for you (at the time of this writing) for just $119.95 at Amazon .com, "steams, blends, defrosts and reheats" your baby's din-dins. Added to which, apparently, it's "easy to clean" and it "preserves vitamins"!

Point Number One: What's wrong with an Adultcook—also known as "an oven"? Most kitchens already have one.

Point Number Two: What's wrong with the shop stuff? Or, when feeling especially energetic, the occasional genu-ine article: mashed-up banana?

I used to watch my girlfriends, ragged with exhaustion, batch steaming bits of broccoli and carrot, mashing them up and putting them into ice cube trays for the freezer. I am not a nutritionist—but everyone knows that food reheated from frozen loses vitamins and taste. (Not that babies have much in the way of taste buds anyway.) So what's the point of it? Why bother?

I did it for a month or so, with baby number one, only because everyone else was doing it: shoved a broccoli stalk in and out of a series of small receptacles and into the freezer. It meant we had no ice cubes, because I never remembered to buy an extra ice cube tray. It meant extra mess and added chores and boredom, time spent fussing around with sauce-pans that could have been spent relaxing in front of the TV. Or learning Portuguese. So I bought some jars—amused myself, mildly, choosing from the truly vast array of flavors available—and never looked back. The baby didn't appear to enjoy the hand-mashed broccoli any more or any less than the jarred stuff—didn't consume any more or less of it, either.

I got to watch a tiny bit more TV and learn a bit more Portuguese. And above all, of course, the baby continued to grow and thrive. *Todos ganha* ("everyone wins"), as I understand they say in Lisbon. *Criança feliz, feliz mãe* ("happy child, happy mother").

For sure, factory-made jars of baby food may work out to be more expensive than the home-cooked variety (if you don't count the opportunity cost of time spent mashing your own broccoli, which could have been spent shorting the market/writing bestsellers/taking in the neighbors' laundry. Also, of course, assuming nobody's invested in a Beaba Babycook Duo Steamer-Blender at $119.95). The cost-saving aspect of home-cooked baby pap is in fact often emphasized by the baby advisers. And I am all for saving money where I can, when it's practical—but we're talking *pennies* here. Babies eat virtually nothing, in any case. Given the phenomenal cost of bringing children into the world, feeding them, clothing them, entertaining them, educating them—the money saved by hand-steaming your own carrots is laughable.

To the experts and the supermoms who prefer to scowl at the jar feeders while smiling nonsensically at their tiny saucepans, I say this:

Steam and mash away, if you want to, but you're making life harder than you need to.

I recommend the Heinz Cheesy Tomato Pasta Stars: $9.50 for ten jars as I write. Just pop in the microwave, Mom (only do take care!).

8. Bedtime, Routines, and Early Starts

Baby number one was subjected to a preposterous "routine": eating and sleeping were monitored and managed to the ounce and to the minute. It was remarkably unrelaxing—and it didn't last for long. Baby number two survived through a muddle of halfhearted routine and drunken confusion due to my father dying shortly after he was born. Baby number three slept and ate whenever she felt like it.

Fast-forward to today. Baby number three is six years old. During the school week she sometimes has to be cajoled into hitting the sack, but during weekends and holidays, like her older siblings, she goes to bed more or less (not entirely) when she likes, and has done so for several years now. Sometimes—often, actually—she conks out on the sofa with the rest of us; sometimes she says, "I'm tired. Please take me to bed." So I do that. It seems to be okay. She has boundless energy. And perhaps because she goes to bed at a civilized hour, she wakes at a reasonably civilized hour, too, allowing her parents to sleep during those precious weekend mornings.

The older ones learned early on how to amuse themselves at antisocial hours of the morning. They learned how to switch on the TV and how to fix themselves a bowl of cereal while their parents slumbered.

This harmless and mutually satisfactory system (the children got to watch all sorts of drivel without being interrupted) only became a source of friction, however, when they were staying with other parents, more fussy or attentive than we were. I don't know why they didn't simply toss the children the remote control. But they didn't. Instead, the parents would cajole all children present into eating appropriate levels of Coco Pops, offer them eggs and freshly squeezed Anywayup cups of organic apple juice.

And the children—well, if somebody *wanted* to offer them fried eggs and chocolate milk, and do coloring and Plasticine and jigsaw puzzles with them at six o'clock in the morning, who were they to argue? Why not?

The commentary would come thick and fast when we two parents finally joined the breakfast party, a stream of unsolicited bulletins—about what our children had eaten or not eaten, how quickly they had been persuaded to get dressed, drink their juice. I longed to cry. My children are *better off* learning to look after themselves. You should've just left them to their own devices and gone back to bed. They would have been fine without you.

9. Bedtime and Alcohol

I read an article over the weekend that suggested readers ask themselves if they were "parentoholics." They were invited to fill in a questionnaire.

Q: What's a parentoholic?

A: It's someone who looks forward to having a glass of wine the moment they put their children to bed.

On closer examination, it's someone who looks forward to having a glass of wine the moment they put their children to bed, and then drinks like a mad fish, wrecks their life as a result, and in all respects behaves like a common or garden-variety alcoholic. Being an alcoholic is clearly a problem. What annoys me is that it should ever have been linked to being a parent who drinks as soon as the children are in bed. What the hell's wrong with that?

My only beef is that we should be expected to wait that long. Do I have a glass of wine as soon as I put the children to bed? Good God, I have one long before! As soon as I turn off the computer. Why? Because I feel like it. Alcohol, for most of us, has a pleasant effect on mood. That's probably a reason why it's so popular. It makes us merrier. And actually, I don't really understand why this is something we feel we should hide from our children. In my experience, children rather prefer it when their parents are merry and relaxed. As indeed (need I add?) do the parents.

Am I a parentoholic? Hard to tell. I drink every day, and with pleasure. Which I think puts a hefty check in the "YES" box. On the other hand, I drink long before the children go to bed—which means I don't run helter-skelter toward the bottle, like a mad thing, the moment they're out of sight. Which I think means a check in the "NO" box. In any case, if I waited until every last one was in bed, I might easily die of thirst.

Being an idle mother who avoids all chores wherever possible, I tend not to find it that taxing having the children around. Quite the opposite, in fact. Which is probably why I rarely insist on them going to bed. In fact, so long as they're not squabbling or creating unnecessary tasks for me, there are no people in the world I feel happier hanging out with.

If you refuse to be a slave for your children and thus resist the temptation to fuss over them or issue them endlessly with non-crucial guidelines and instructions—and if you insist that they repay such thoughtfulness by not issuing *you* with non-crucial chores—then there won't be such a parental sense of being "on duty" when the children are up and about, and parents won't feel like they are "off duty" when the children finally go to bed. And the frantic "parentoholic" rush to hit the bottle, come the end of the day, is reduced to altogether more seemly levels of gentle enthusiasm.

N.B.: Obviously, with children under two and a half years old, this system doesn't work so well. At this early stage, when children are still so helpless, it's impossible to relax much while they're still up and impossible not to feel relieved when they finally go to bed. Not to worry! Though it's hard to imagine it at the time, *this phase of family life will pass.* A few years of more full-throttle parentoholism may be unavoidable: until the children are old enough to take themselves to the bathroom, pour themselves a glass of water, go upstairs, and put their own pajamas on, let's say—after which point, evening drinking can once again be approached with a little more moderation and elegance.

10. Sex

I think of those sorry Victorian women with their twenty-five children each, half of whom didn't survive beyond the first year of life, and I am filled with pity, almost as much as I am filled with wonder. How did they manage it? We all know getting pregnant isn't nearly as easy as we claim it is to our teenage children. Those Victorians must have been at it, shagging like bunny rabbits by the candlelight, night after night, year in and year out.

We tell each other so many lies about how often we have sex: when, why, how satisfactorily, and with whom. Nevertheless, it's a truth universally acknowledged that modern parents of young children don't have sex with each other that much. It's for all sorts of reasons: we can say it's because "the kids might walk in" until we are blue in the face, but, as many will recall from their dim and distant past, where there's a will, there tends to be a way.

Mostly, what with one thing and another, exhausted from all that overwork and overparenting, modern parents often aren't all that attracted to each other. Something happens between couples when they've spent too many of their leisure hours saying to each other:

"Have I got puke on my back?"

"But you went to the gym yesterday, it's my turn."

"Am I leaking?"

"I changed him last time."

"No, *no*. Not like that. No, oh God . . . it doesn't matter. Forget it. I'll do it."

A little of the magic fades away. How could it not? When children are very young, parents can sometimes feel like caged animals, pacing our baby-proofed hutches: bound together by pastel-colored plastics, feeding routines, sugary-smelling diaper wipes, and a wretched shortage of funds. It's hard, from time to time, not to mistake our fellow cellmate for a jailer.

It's a dreadful state of affairs, and it's remarkable that so many partnerships survive at all. You've been breathing the same air, negotiating the same chores all day. Add to that, yes, there is the constant threat of a child barging in on the act. No matter how much you loved and desired each other once—and may yet again—for the moment at least, the chances are you are to each other the anti-aphrodisiac.

If neither party much wants to have sex with the other, is it reasonable or sensible to insist, along with all the other restrictions their shared situation necessarily imposes, that they don't at least entertain the idea of having sex with someone else? I'm not advocating open relationships, God forbid. I'm just not *not* advocating them, either.

Part III

Child Care

Because Easygoing Parenting
Saves You Time and Money
and Is Good for the Whole Family

1. Unparenting

It's annoying, isn't it, when you think you've had an original idea and then it turns out someone else has already come up with it. I have just discovered an exciting and fast-growing new parenting movement called "unparenting." As you might discern from its name, unparenting promotes a hands-off approach to child rearing—nonprescriptive, engaged, affectionate, fluid, open-minded, adaptable, liberal, mutually respectful: to which admirable mix I would inject only a defiant shot of feminism. And suggest *mutually gratifying*. It's a modern truism, as discussed, that motherhood should be a one-way street, a no-right-of-way relationship structured for the kiddies' benefit and for the kiddies' alone. But that's unrealistic. It's silly, sentimental, anti-female. And creepy.

Although it is galling to learn that I am just another voice in a growing movement, it is exhilarating to discover that I'm not, after all, on my own out here, crying freedom and common sense on the playground. If others are coming to the same—or similar—conclusions, there is hope for the future yet. Don't misunderstand me: "unparenting" does not mean surrendering my role as first-port-of-call parent. Absolutely not!

I get heartache if I am to spend a night away from my children. I get heartache *several days in the run-up to the separation*. In fact—it probably sounds weak, but it's hardly unusual—I get (slight) heartache if I know, in the morning, that I won't make it home in time to see them before they go to bed. Mother love—it's an affliction (or sometimes it feels that way) that fades, I sincerely hope, when the children grow up and leave the nest.

By unparenting, I mean that we avoid making motherhood any more wearisome, costly, or complicated than it needs to be. It means banishing pointless after-school activities that entail chauffeuring; eliminating "playdates" that require organizing more than a couple of days in advance; no more costume requirements for school shows and assemblies; and definitely no more maternal guilt.

2. Guilt

Several years back, a nasty dose of maternal guilt drove me briefly to join the Stay-at-Home league of mothers. I got rid of the child care, we moved to the country, and for a year I did almost no paid work at all. I baked cakes, attended coffee mornings, cooked wholesome dinners for my children, examined the local wildlife, and watched an amazing amount of TV.

It wasn't simply the change in my finances that was difficult. In fact, for much of that time, I was still being paid for work I had completed before my somewhat premature retirement. As any newly unemployed person will tell you, it was the loss of all the things I had previously taken for granted: independence, intellectual stimulation, a sense of personal achievement, identity, and status. Also the unwelcome emergence of a sudden, horrifying reliance on the other half, not yet for money (though that would come), but for news and contact with the rest of the world. We had started out, he and I, before all this maternal angst had led us to the green fields, as equals and friends in the great adventure of life. In a matter of months I had transformed into a cartoon of the discontented housewife.

We lived in a lovely house (perfect for the kids) in a well-to-do corner of this green and pleasant land, within an hour or so of London. It was high-priced commuter land. During the week, while the menfolk went off to work, I lived, as full-time mothers tend to, in a world peopled only by women, every one of us on the same small treadmill. We talked about the kids and worried about the kids and talked about the kids and talked about what was best for the kids and talked about what was not best for the kids. At a stroke, my universe had shrunk to nothing but the school and the house. Everything beyond had simply disappeared.

I began to resent my husband's access to the wider world, felt jealous of his business trips away. Quite soon, aware of how little I had to say to the still-toiling girlfriends I had left behind, I lost the confidence to make contact with them. It was the loneliest—and actually the most boring—year of my life. I tried in earnest to be the sort of mother I thought I was meant to be—fulfilled by the delights of motherhood and of motherhood alone—and I came up against a major obstacle. Me.

Plenty of women offered counsel and comfort; plenty understood. Oh God, it's hell, they agreed. But, they added, you get used it. It takes about five years (weirdly, a time period they all seemed independently to have agreed upon). The first five years are really tough. But after that you get used to it. These days, they said, I honestly wouldn't have it any other way.

I was lucky. Being self-employed, I had a clear route out of the situation. Added to which, for some reason, I've never been particularly embarrassed about saying that I've screwed up. Which I clearly had.

Several years later a well-known radio presenter, a doyenne of feminism, or so I had always assumed, asked me during a live broadcast of her show if I felt guilty about dragging the family back to London after our failed adventure. I am still infuriated by the question. A family can be only as happy as its least happy member, I told her. But I wish I had said more. Or less, actually. The point is, I was miserable and that should be enough. Would she have asked my husband if he felt guilty? Would she have asked my children, if they were the ones who had been suffering? I suspect not. Mothers are expected to put up with their personal wretchedness so long as the rest of the family is happy. That is cruel and archaic nonsense.

I know of another family who made a similar move from London to the country around the same time; the man commuted, the woman became a housewife and was miserable. When she confided her unhappiness, her husband said: "But this move isn't about you. It's about the kids." She was foolish enough to believe him, and though she wears a brave face, it is painfully obvious that she is still miserable today. It's too bad. It fills me with rage, actually.

Anyway, we moved back to London rather poorer than we had left it, what with all the buying and selling of houses. The children returned to their old school. I returned to my writing desk.

3. More Guilt
(To Work or Not to Work?)

Fathers don't feel it. Why do we? Somewhere along the line modern mothers have accepted guilt as an inevitable part of the parenting package, as if guilt were the price we have to pay for equality and choice. But it makes not a jot of sense. We give life; we feed, clothe, comfort, and protect; we care for our children the best we can; lavish on them our unconditional, absolute, everlasting love—and yet we feel it is not enough: because in this neurotic excessive-parenting culture, nothing will ever be enough—nothing short of a sort of maternal suttee.

It means we tend to feel a little divided and are perhaps not as straightforward as we could be when it comes to the thorny matter of careers or paid work.

My husband, our three children, and I lead a comfortable, middle-class life in one of the most expensive cities in the world. By any reasonable standards, we are well-off. The money I earn probably makes up a third of our household income, and without it much in our household, including the house itself, would have to change. But do I have to work, or is it a choice?

Working mothers tend to begin all discussions on this tricky subject from the defensive premise that they don't have any choice in the matter.

What I am about to say won't go down too well. Nevertheless, I've got to say it, because our attitudes toward work are so entwined with our maternal guilt and martyrdom. The fact is, many of us do have a choice.

Most stay-at-home mothers in Britain, as least, will never starve, nor will their children. We have free education, we have the National Health Service, and we have a welfare state specifically to prevent such a thing from happening. Once her children are of school age, a mother may be teased and bullied into going on a handful of unwanted job interviews, but she can botch them if she wants to. She and her children will certainly live in poverty, but they will not be destitute. It will never be a matter of life and death. Which means working mothers in Britain—single, unsupported mothers without a bean to their name, as well as mothers currently hitched to an earning other, as well as lucky cows like me— go to work because we prefer it to the alternative. We work because we want to. This is just as true of a fair number of mothers elsewhere, even in the United States.

Say it out loud. "I work because I want to work: because I prefer it to the alternative; for autonomy, independence, self-respect; in some cases, for personal enjoyment; and, above all, for cash. I go to work and earn a living because it's preferable to staying at home and, in the long run, more gratifying."

Many of us working mothers make quite a hullabaloo about how exhausting it is to be us: all that juggling and baking cakes at midnight. Well, even if it is exhausting (which it is), most of us will say, in private, and assuming it hasn't been a spectacularly bad day at work, that almost any level of exhaustion-while-juggling is preferable to the powerless, confined, stay-at-home alternative. Pretty much anything is probably better, as most men would agree, than a life of unpaid domestic drudgery and dependency, in a world that rarely extends beyond the kitchen and the school gate.

So I sent out a tweet (nothing like doing a bit of research) asking the mothers out there to share their thoughts: Did they work and wish they didn't, or vice versa? Were they happy with the choices they had made?

There were bits and bobs of frothing self-righteousness from the evangelical stay-at-home brigade (the same women, I imagine, who a hundred years ago might have joined the Women's National Anti-Suffrage League) and a clutch of replies from the middle ground: nonworkers' replies were more plentiful, more wistful, and less certain. Replies from workers were more succinct and sounded more confident. But almost all of them dwelled on maternal guilt:

"I work p-t, have 3 kids (6, 5, 3). Feel guilty about being happy to go to work after 5 yrs at home."

"I've worked full-time, part-time, and stayed at home. Staying at home def the hardest, but felt guilty with all of them."

"Nonworkng Mom. Feel guilty about unfulfilled ambition/ guilt for no plan now kids getting older. What next?"

The guilt is everywhere: insidious and self-defeating. Obviously, or it seems obvious to me, we should fight it. Shouldn't we? At least stop measuring our performance altogether and just get on with it, confident that our self-respect and instinct for survival, and the ordinary, natural, irrepressible love we feel for our children, will help us muddle through, allow us to raise our beloved children the best we can, and, along the way, to reclaim whatever we might of ourselves: not simply as mothers but as adults, equals and individuals in a shared universe.

It's a particular form of torture, leaving our babies and toddlers behind. No matter where it is, or with whom—a grandmother, a nanny, a day care center. The sound of their cries is horrible. Visceral, like someone pouring vinegar into the veins. But there are dividends. And as we all know, those heartbreaking cries pass very quickly.

"She'll be fine in a minute," the caregiver says, clutching our bawling baby, silently longing for us to leave already and stop protracting the wretched scene. "Don't you worry," they say. "She'll be laughing in a second." And of course we know it's true. There'll be other babies to goggle at, innumerable bits of brightly colored plastic to amuse. She'll have something else to distract her—feeding the ducks, perhaps.

The point is, either way, within a couple of minutes or less, those bloodcurdling cries will have turned to gentle hiccups, and until we cross their eyeline again, our babies will have more or less forgotten we exist.

It's wonderful to feel needed, one of the great pulls and pleasures of motherhood. But let's not get above ourselves. Feeding the ducks is feeding the ducks, no matter who's holding out the bag of stale bread.

The idea that women should want to fill their days watching over their children so very intensively is really very new: a faintly degenerate invention to fill the domestic void created by washing machines. Until my own mother's generation, upper- and middle-class women (anyone, frankly, who could afford it) employed nannies and nursery maids to do most of the grunt work for them, the same work that modern mothers are supposed to find so fulfilling. Working-class women, overloaded by grunt work already, had more pressing demands on their time, as well as extended family and (before the community-wrecking apartment blocks) neighbors long known to one another around and about to help keep an open eye.

Modern mothers walk a tightrope of tact. Aware of how inadequate we all feel, we tend to keep our own counsel on the delicate matter of which is preferable: to work or not to work. Everyone is different, we say. "Female empowerment" is all about, well, not being mean to each other, applauding one another no matter what, never really saying anything controversial.

To work or not to work? I may be wrong (I suppose), but imagine that you could take maternal guilt completely out of the equation. If you knew that your children were in good hands, if you could work but with balance, not excessively, and cover your child care costs with something left over, and assuming the work wasn't actively unpleasant, then for so many of us it would have to be a no-brainer. Self-sufficiency and independence and a connection with the wider world breed confidence and self-respect, which breeds good cheer.

Since recent studies can say whatever you want them to say, and there really appears to be no conclusive evidence to suggest that the children of full-time mothers fare any better than their more neglected but equally adored playmates, you have to ask yourself: When life is so short and the world is so wide, and confidence and independence and earning money feel so good, what's to stay at home *for*?

Added to which, the more working mothers there are, the fewer nonworking mothers there will be, which means fewer well-intentioned but inessential tasks concocted to fill the days, which the rest of us have to run around desperately trying to find time to do, or desperately apologize for failing to do. It would mean fewer notes home from school asking for home-baked cakes for the cake stand and homemade play dough for the nursery; fewer exhortations to attend midweek, early afternoon singing/swimming/dancing shows. Unnecessary parental input will, by necessity, be pared to a sensible minimum, and the children themselves will be left in peace, in their carefree, childlike paradise, to make the hats, bake the cakes, and do their frigging homework for themselves.

It's a win-win.

"My name is D., I have three children, and for a long time, until a few months ago, I employed full-time help with house and children. Financially, it was a killer, but at the time it made sense. Now that the children are older, they can help to look after each other and we muddle through. It's fine."

Over the years, depending on the ages of the children and what money was coming in, I have experimented with most child care options available: day care drop-in, nanny-share, live-out au pair, live-in au pair, take-it-in-turns with another parent, mix 'n' match all of the above. And out in the country, for one year only, no child care at all. Whatever worked, or worked well enough, simply had to do. No arrangement was perfect.

People sometimes politely asked me, as they do all working mothers: How on earth do you manage? When I said, "Well, I have a lot of help," they often looked rather surprised. Sometimes even a little embarrassed. But how the hell else would I get any work done? Every mother of young children who works has to use help—for which, at some point, unless she happens to be among the fortunate few blessed with a saintly relative willing to step in absolutely free, money, or payment in kind, must change hands.

And yet, somehow, the obvious truth of this—working mothers' fundamental dependence on outsourcing their child care—remains slightly shameful. So it is mean, and a little cowardly, when high-profile women refuse to lead the way, come clean, and admit to all the help they have. And of all the high-profile women who would like us to believe they raise their children in a cloud of gravity-defying magic dust, Michelle Obama may be the most infuriating culprit.

Her children are older now, but she has always told us that she doesn't employ a nanny, perhaps because the First Grandma moved into the White House along with the First Family. Except I don't suppose the First Grandma sews the name tags in the clothes, does she? Or checks that the right clothes are ready and ironed for school the following morning, or goes to the drugstore to stock up on lice eradicator— time-consuming child care duties, each and every one. And if Granny's not doing it, and Michelle's not doing it, and we must all hope Barack has something more pressing to do with his time, then who do you suppose is? Call him/her what you will: a Harvard Business School "civil servant" or a good old-fashioned maid. Does the fact that somebody else in the Obama household stocks up on Band-Aids and Tylenol make Michelle a less loving mother? Hardly. But the fact that she's not straightforward about what it takes for her to play a part in the wider world, that she won't speak up about working mothers' dependence on child care, makes her a less than perfect feminist, without a doubt.

5. The Unspoken Battle

It's called the "mommy wars" in the media, which is patronizing but not inaccurate. It's the delicate and unwinnable battle between the mothers who go out to work and the mothers who don't. Mostly, we keep a fragile truce. We try our best to get along. But beneath the smiles and grimaces and apologies, there is a small bubbling cauldron of mutual distrust and resentment. No doubt my earlier reference to "inessential tasks" won't much help to ease the peace between the two camps, either. It was annoying of me.

The difficulty, of course, is that by the mere fact of their existence, each group undermines the strivings of the other. If a woman can be a good mother and also hold down a job, then what the hell are the full-time mothers doing with themselves all day? On the other hand, obviously, if there really is enough mothering to be done that it can fill an entire existence, could it mean the children of working mothers are missing out?

I was discussing the incredibly fragile truce that exists between the earning and nonearning factions with two other mothers, clever, reasonable, decent women both (under normal circumstances). Both had young children and full-time jobs. The conversation started well enough:

. . . Oh dear, yes, it is a minefield isn't it. . . . [or something along these lines]

You feel you're being rude when you're not available to help out with things . . . so you're endlessly having to apologize . . .

. . . and endlessly having to say thank you . . .

. . . and then they say "not to worry" and of course they're only being helpful—but you want to say, Well, but I wouldn't have to "worry" if only you'd stop creating so many pointless tasks for me to do. . . .

At which point the conversation took a turn. "Sometimes, on my way to work," one of us declared, "I walk past the mothers in their gym clothes, sitting around having coffee with each other, and I want to pick up their frigging cappuccinos and pour them on their heads.

"I sometimes fantasize about hooking them up onto some kind of electrical circuit and turning up the voltage so their hair stands on end. It might wipe the smug look off their faces just for a second."

It was just a moment, a nasty little moment at the end of a long week, born of insecurity, no doubt, and irritability and jealousy and pack behavior and let's call it "juggle fatigue." Plus, it was quite funny. I have no doubt that, from time to time, the other side feels no less ferocious about us as they stand under a tent in the playground in the pouring rain, manning the National Reading Week Tuesday Lunchtime book-exchange stall. I'm sure they would dearly love to take our self-important BlackBerrys and shove them where the sun don't shine.

What happens to a full-time mother when her children finally leave home? Perhaps her spouse, assuming there is one, retires from his job at the same time? And perhaps, despite her long-standing withdrawal from a world beyond her children's, she still has plenty to say that's worth listening to and the two still have some things in common, other than the love of their fully grown children? And perhaps they have money to spare (though how, I don't quite know, with only half the household bringing it in) and perhaps they buy a round-trip ticket to see the world together. How lovely.

And then what? She's still young: in her fifties, probably. It's a lot of years to live without having anything much to do. Sometimes I look at our family-sized house and imagine it empty, as it will be when the children have all flown the nest. And I am awash with misery. Nothing could ever fill the void—all the life and hope and merriment they bring to the place. But at least, as long as I am working, there will be something to keep me occupied when they have left—and, better yet, a reason that requires me to stay engaged with the world.

Everyone I know goes away in the end, as the song goes. But our children are certainly supposed to go away eventually. Better to make like a Boy Scout. Be prepared. Have a life.

6. Soppy Dads

How is it that some people—British people in particular, perhaps?—having procreated with (arguably) some degree of success, feel they no longer have even the faintest duty to remain if not alluring then at least not repugnant to the other sex? I ask the question about women, so many of whom seem to surrender their sexuality at the altar of mommydom.

But at least with women, you can understand how it comes about—what with the process of pregnancy and birth, breaking waters, leaking breasts, and torn vaginas, not to mention breast-feeding, vomit wiping, etc., etc.—that these things can bend the old self-image out of shape. Just a tad. Feeling like a sexual being again after all that takes, for most of us, time, sleep, and also a concerted effort. But the men? The Soppy Dad Brigade—soft-voiced and squeaky-soled, who seem to grow bosoms as their partners' baby bump develops, who sit on the floor in communal prenatal classes, empathizing their way through the pelvic floor exercises . . . What's their excuse? *What happened to them?* Were they like that at school? Was that the face they wore when they were courting the future mothers of their children? Or did they just gulp back too much estrogen in the tap water in the intervening period? It raises a question (or it does to me): How did they ever get laid in the first place?

You see them everywhere, the Soppy Dad Brigade: at parental get-togethers, and wandering the aisles of supermarkets, and—occasionally—even married to friends. They talk to their children in special voices, often (which isn't simply irritating; it's bloody creepy) referring to themselves in the third person: "Daddy wants you to sit at the table and eat your carrot pap. What did Daddy tell you earlier? Daddy's getting a teeny bit angry now. . . ."

I like to imagine Daddy much later, when the other adults are gone, and the kiddies are safely tucked up in bed, and Daddy's not a teeny bit angry anymore; he is on his own, soft-soled sandals warming by the natural-gas fire, relaxing, at last, in the safe, early evening. While Mommy's upstairs, rubbing soothing gel into her well-worn nipples, feeling slightly smug, perhaps, about the broken husk of a man she shares her bed with every night, Soppy Hubby is downstairs in the living room, jacking off feverishly to online porn . . . possibly involving fluffy animals. I sort of hope he is. For everyone's sake, really. But mostly for my own peace of mind. Somebody's got to be watching that stuff, after all. Let's imagine it's him.

7. Stay-at-Home Dads

Are not the same as Soppy Dads. In fact, I think it takes a certain amount of courage, on the part of *both* parents, to travel along this still quite unconventional pathway. At my children's schools and nurseries at least, there have always been at least a couple of househusbands on duty—more, I note, since the recession. Some are only passing through, between redundancies, putting on a brave face. Others are there for the duration. In either case, they tend to cut rather solitary figures at the gates, though this may also be out of choice.

Some of the stay-at-home-mother brigade are prone to treating them with a mysteriously chilly disdain, I've noticed: ferociously unflirtatious, as if they were sort of half-men, and often addressing them slowly, as they might someone else's not-immediately-useful au pair, with a memsahib-ish mixture of dislike, distrust, impatience, and incomprehension. I am not sure why this is. Perhaps these women feel their turf is being threatened. Or that their roles as financially dependent wives and mothers are being somehow under-mined by such a grotesque perversion of the natural order. Who knows what it is about househusbands that annoy them so. But something clearly does.

8. Feeding Children

• Healthy Snacks

It's hard enough getting from A to B with a toddler at the best of times, bearing in mind how slowly they walk, how little they understand the concept of time or deadlines or the word "hurry" or the importance of remembering where they left their shoes. In the winter, there's likely to be an added fifteen minutes of preparation time before leaving the house, helping them with coats and gloves and hats. And then, depending on duration and distance of the journey ahead, there will be *luggage*. Truckloads of the stuff: diapers and baby wipes, plastic toys and pacifiers, strollers and rain covers and high chairs and sun hats and car seats and sunblock and portable cribs and teddy bears and backup T-shirts and diaper bags and washcloths—in fact, just thinking about it makes me want to weep with gratitude and joy that my children have outgrown all that.

Why, then, would any mother want to add to these sometimes seemingly insurmountable obstacles by making the process of getting out of the house any more difficult than it already is? And yet.

What is it with those little Tupperware snack boxes? It's as if children under three years old can't travel to the bus stop, can't walk across their own bloody living rooms, without a hygienically packaged healthy snackette—if not already in their mouth, at least within immediate reach of it.

You see them everywhere: in other people's cars and other people's kitchens, in other people's handbags and wedged between the handlebars of other people's strollers: EZ-open, EZ-cleen, toddler-safe, airtight, snap-shut, germ-free, teeny-tiny plastic tubs, filled with precut carrot bits. Little slices of apple. Miniature bread sticks. And I am bewildered.

A toddler's snack in a toddler snack box is simply one more thing to carry, prepare, clean, leave behind on public transportation, gather dust in the backseat of a car, or rot at the bottom of a handbag. It's one more thing for a child to whine about. And it's completely unnecessary.

Children aren't like sheep and horses (and possibly elephants?). They don't need to graze all day long.

• Juice

See above. "Juice" is good for treats. But for everyday it strikes me as somewhat excessive. It's an extra cost, an extra weight in a shopping basket, an extra space in a cupboard, an extra thing to run out of, an extra thing to prepare in the general rigmarole of feeding children. It's fattening, tooth-rotting, and actually (as with the constant-need-for-healthy-snack-in-mouth scenario above) there's something vaguely effete about small children whining for "juice" with their dinner that makes me want to prod them sharply (when the parents aren't looking) and whisper a single word: *Spoiled*.

What's wrong with tap water?

• Fussy Eating

Remember the olden days, when the adults still had hang-ups about clean plates? They used to whip themselves into frenzies of puritanical irritation when confronted by their children's delicate palates and fussy eating habits. It was a *thing* that united every adult, apparently. No matter what color, creed, or background. Children had to be made to clean their plates. No matter what.

Most of us have been at the receiving end of the older generation's clean-plate fetish at some point, I'm sure. I know I have. At home, with my gourmand parents, over Jerusalem artichokes and lovage soups and . . . never mind. At school, alone in the dining hall after everyone had left, gagging and weeping over tapioca, banana custard, tepid semolina with dried skin on top. The background strum was just the same: *waste not, want not/think of the starving Africans/you don't know how lucky you are . . .* The thought of lovage soup, by the way, still makes my stomach heave.

Anyway, it's probably because those of my generation endured similar scenes in their childhood that we tend to be so gentle—not to say indulgent—of our own children's nutritional peccadilloes. I don't know anyone anymore who forces their children to finish food they actively dislike. I certainly don't.

On the other hand, I don't offer them a "menu choice," either. It's troublesome enough preparing one "meal option," for heaven's sake, let alone an array of them. So they can eat what's on offer—or they can not eat it. If they don't eat it, they'll probably be hungry and will make up for it later. Or they can fill up on bread, which is nice and cheap. It doesn't really matter, and I don't really care. They certainly aren't going to starve.

• Organic Food

Is a waste of money. Studies have shown. Or some studies have shown. Enough, anyway, to persuade me not to bother.

A bit like novels with "Short-listed for the Booker" on the front. If a food has "organic" on the label, I take care to leave it on the shelf.

9. Allergies, Intolerances, and Other Health Alerts

One of my children is slightly allergic to peaches. Her lips swell up and her throat itches. Or, rather, that's what used to happen. I eventually took her to the doctor, who did a test, and who informed us that she was also allergic to hazelnuts, which she wasn't really. And after that, I don't know quite what happened. . . . Peaches aren't something that feature too large in an ordinary northern European's diet. The impetus to resolve the "problem" sort of faded away.

We were meant to go and see a further consultant, who would tell us what else she was allergic to, but we never quite got around to it. I said, "Maybe you shouldn't eat peaches. Or hazelnuts," which suggestions she chose to ignore. Now the peach allergy has gone, and the hazelnut allergy continues to travel incognito, if it travels at all; and everything seems to be okay. The end.

Great story, eh? (There's nothing quite like an unsolicited food intolerance tale to get the old heart beating.) Anyway. Some allergies are all too real. Clearly. (With a nod to my lovely godson.) But you can't help wondering whether some may possibly be a teeny-tiny bit more real than others. I'm just saying, once you venture down the ask-a-consultant-why-my-kid's-a-bit-whiny route, it can be quite hard to turn back. The initial "he has a tummy ache when he eats stuff that's chewy" may soon turn into an obstacle course, riddled with unnecessary challenges: weeks and months tussling with doctor appointments personnel, followed, eventually, by lists of previously unsuspected problems and disorders—and of hazelnuts better avoided. Children grow out of most allergies naturally, and if there's anything better to avoid in life—all walks of life—it's lists of things better avoided.

10. Seeing the Doctor

The physical state of any family member needs to be grim indeed if it's driven us to join the snuffling, deadweight inertia of a doctor's office.

Hell, they are depressing places. Aren't they, though?

First, there's the demoralizing period in the reception room, waiting politely to be seen. We never know how long this period will last, and yet, inexplicably, it seems rude to ask. Since these rooms are usually brimming with feverish children with hacking coughs and anxious mothers pecking at their smartphones, it's quite difficult to remain in one for long without losing the will to live, thereby rather defeating the purpose of the entire excursion.

Then there's that dizzyingly brief moment when you and your child are actually allowed in to see the doctor. *Tappety-tap* at the keyboard, goes the doc, hardly pausing to look up from his/her computer screen. What-seems-to-be-the-problem? *Tappety-tap* . . .

But when it comes to the usual array of childish (or adult) afflictions, there's rarely much they can do to help, is there?

"Viral," they say. "If it hasn't cleared up in a few days, then come back." *Tappety-tap*. And we say, politely gathering our coats: *Come on, darling! Time to go! Say thank you to the doctor!* And off we waddle home again. Half a morning wasted.

And in a couple of days, lo and behold: the childish affliction . . . clears up.

Family doctors, let's face it, are often *slightly* useless. Unless there's something serious going on. Or unless you happen to be someone who describes minor health symptoms to health professionals for simple reassurance. And, actually, I've begun to realize there are plenty of people out there who do just that. In any case, I am not one of them. If an ailment is going to get better anyway, as most do, it's hard to see the point of making a journey to somewhere incredibly depressing to discuss it with someone who almost certainly won't be able to help. Take some ibuprofen and wait two days. Save time—yours, your child's, and the doctor's.

11. Mother's Day

My mother decreed that it was soppy, sentimental nonsense, mercilessly exploited—possibly even invented—by greedy purveyors of expensive soaps and decent chocolates. So we were never encouraged to celebrate Mother's Day as children.

Clearly, that was a mistake. It should be milked for all it's worth.

12. Father's Day

Soppy, sentimental nonsense, mercilessly exploited—possibly even invented—by greedy purveyors of useless sporting accessories and presidential biographies. I don't think we can get away with ignoring it altogether without risking a reduction of services in the reciprocal event. Nevertheless—a child's hand-drawn card or something similar ought, I feel, to be more than enough.

13. Fathers and Daughters

The only time I feel a real surge of truly old-fashioned feminist dislike for the other sex is when I hear them talk in coy, facetious horror about the prospect of their young daughters one day forming relationships with men. It's a convention, isn't it—even for the Soppy Dad Brigade—to make cutesy, He-Man noises of protest about the future sexual relations of their precious girls. "No man will be good enough!" they declare. "I swear, no man's ever going near her." *Chuckle, chuckle,* go the dinner guests. *How sweet!* These protestations are meant to convey, in deprecating and humorous fashion, the immeasurable love and esteem a father has for his little girl. And perhaps they do convey that. But if so, what do they convey about the love and esteem he has for all the other women in his life? His wife, for example? The He-Man declarations take as understood that no loving father would wish upon his daughter what he himself has wished upon all the women he ever loved and desired. And there's nothing terribly sweet about that. Sounds psychopathic to me.

And worryingly conceited, too, since these declarations pivot on the assumption that, in heterosexual relationships, all men exploit all women; and that women, no matter what, will always emerge the losers.

Dream on, fellas.

14. Birthday Parties

They've become laughably competitive; in my rich corner of the world, the extent to which parents will go to outshine one another is beyond parody. I know of children whose parents have flown half a class of children to Disneyland Paris for the weekend; I know of one ten-year-old whose parents rented a suite at the Savoy for all the girls in the class and booked a couple of professional makeup artists as entertainment for a "makeover-'n'-sleepover party." I know of parents who have rented out private movie theaters, so that their children can watch a special early screening of a film that's yet to be released. All of which, I realize, is extreme—a symptom of the vulgar wealth sloshing around in London private schools. Bring on the revolution.

Nevertheless, the drive to make one's children's birthday parties more special, more memorable, more extravagant than anyone else's is not only a frailty of the extortionately rich. I promised myself when I set out to write this book that I would never use the words "in my day" and "we were perfectly all right."

However—

In my day, we had a few people over, some Jell-O and Hula Hoops, a pass-the-parcel (with a SINGLE present in the center, not one at every layer), a pin-the-tail-on-the-donkey, some musical statues. Birthday cake. Maybe a balloon to take home. Thank you for having me. Time to go home. And that was it. And it was better than perfectly all right. It was wonderful. Especially the Jell-O.

It takes nerves of steel to pull off anything so simple today. Even basic birthday parties at home (as opposed to the ones in cripplingly expensive theme parks, paintball arenas, etc.) seem to involve kiddie-friendly party wranglers in kiddie-friendly clown clothes at $150 to $300 a pop or DJs with glitter on their faces. And what with the themed party bags, matching themed party stationery, themed bloody birthday cake—the cost of these little get-togethers can sky-rocket. It's madness, I tell you!

Why do we do it? Children's birthday parties are only meant to be a bit of fun.

How do we stop? Well, now—

We just stop.

I gave a fourth-birthday party for one of my children several years ago. I had "organized" the party myself—*sans* the $300 entertainer—and, I'll be honest, it was anarchy. I was desperate. Nobody wanted to play the party games. Or sit down to tea, or whatever it was they were meant to be doing. A girlfriend of mine, there for moral support—who didn't have children at the time—said, "Oh, just put some music on and tell them to dance." So I did. And the children danced . . . and danced . . . and danced. And then they had some birthday cake. And then they went home and lived happily ever after.

Small children couldn't care less what's laid on, so long as something is and they're at the center of it. So long as there's Jell-O and a couple of prizes and everyone sings "Happy Birthday" and makes them feel special. Older children may not want musical chairs and Jell-O, but whatever they do want, if it's expensive it can be done with a single friend, not in a bloody great group. Apart from the fact that such lavish parties are unnecessary and unaffordable, I think they're kind of gross. Because spoiled children are gross. And so are their parents.

A friend of mine just forwarded me a party invitation addressed to her six-year-old son. Party guests are advised to bring "strong shoes or boots" as they will be walking "approximately 50 yards" between feasting table and small park, for the party games.

"We will be enough adults," the birthday boy's mother adds at the bottom of the invitation, *"to satisfy Department of Health requirements for adult to child ratio for the walk down* ☺*."*

Oh, it's all so joyless! It's so cautious! It's so inelegant! It's so unutterably *pathetic*. What has become of us all? Who gives a damn what satisfies the Department of Health? It's a private party! And it makes me want to emigrate.

15. Other People's Children

Are likely to be fractionally less interesting and more irritating to us than our own, and the younger and more whiny they are, the more adamantly this tends to be the case. Other people's children do, however, have an important role, no matter what their age, because they often make our own children very happy. Also, by the mistakes they make while visiting our houses, they can throw a useful light on how our own children, so fascinating, fragile, and delightful to us, might themselves be slightly annoying while visiting the houses of others.

Other people's children, I hasten to add (yours, especially) are often genuinely adorable. But they do start from a disadvantage. What we like to call "confidence" in our own children can come across, in others, more like a deluded sense of entitlement.

Children are inclined to be solipsistic at the best of times. They can't help that, due to being young and inexperienced. But modern parenting, with its "our kiddie-king is self-expressing" approach, seems, unhelpfully, to encourage the skewed vision rather than attempt to put it right.

Our children have been encouraged to function under the false assumption that every adult in their orbit—with the possible exception of the numerous pedophiles roaming outside every candy store—has their interests, personal comfort, and immediate pleasure uppermost in their hearts and minds. Hence the occasional unsolicited bulletins from visiting children, when presented with a plate of food, as to how much they're probably not going to like it.

"I hope s/he likes chicken nuggets," mothers used to say to me, when they were having one of my children to dinner. "Because if s/he doesn't like chicken nuggets, we can easily toss in a couple of extra sausages. It's no trouble at all."

"For heaven's sake," I wanted cry, "he'll probably like the nuggets or maybe he won't—and then he'll go without."

I don't expect much from the children who visit us; they come, they go: they are always welcome. Some are cute—there's an extra-cute one on the landing outside the door, giggling about stolen cookies, as I write this. I'm very fond of some of them: embarrassingly so, my children would probably say. In any case, it's a lovely surprise when they grow a little older and engage in conversation. It's a nuisance, when they're young, if they occasionally smash things, or finish all the cookies, or stay up half the night, bouncing footballs in the hall, or making pancakes, or flooding the bathroom, or scribbling art on the walls. Generally, of course, they don't. And if they do, it's not the end of the world. Far from it. It may be a nuisance, but it's also part of the merry chaos of life, and—so long as nobody expects anyone to provide an alternative or do anything in particular for them at all, really, except vacate the TV room and (see "Sleepovers," below) direct them to the closet where we keep the sleeping bags—it's a pleasure to have them over.

However, as they leave the house, trail of empty cookie tins and pizza boxes behind them, there ought to be some sort of a checklist for child guests. Stop, look at me, and say: "Good-bye and thank you." It's all I want. In exchange for quite so many cookies, it seems like a small request.

Part IV

School

1. Nursery School

Funny how important it seemed to get the children into the best one—rather, the one everyone else, somewhat randomly (it always struck me), agreed was "the best." Because looking back at them all now, years later—the ones I looked at and didn't apply to, the ones I fought and groveled to get my children into—I can hardly tell them apart. Lots of little tables and scruffy boxes of well-used toys; a handful of kindly teachers (except for you, Miss A——); a classroom filled with other small children to entertain and befriend one another; and a bonus point for a pet rabbit.

A nursery school, above all, is somewhere to leave the toddler for a couple of hours each morning so that his mother can begin to remember what it's like to be a human again: the sort of human who, for example, is free to amble to the bathroom without a ten-minute hazard analysis of the health and safety implications of leaving a toddler alone in the living room.

Some schools may have shinier toys, of course. Some may teach your child to write her name earlier than others.

(What's the rush?) But when you get down to it, they're all pretty much the same! The only thing that really matters is that the place is nearby, as near as possible. Those precious three hours spin past: faster than time ever has or ever will again. Spend it traveling backward and forward to the "best" nursery school—and you may yet run out of time for that longed-for impulse trip to the bathroom.

2. First Day: Having a Little Cry

I have forgotten when mothers are officially expected to do this. When a child starts at nursery school or when a child leaves to go to a big school? Personally, I don't remember "having a little cry" at either end of this incredibly minor chapter in a child's life, except—yes, perhaps a brief smarting of relief when I realized I would never again have to be polite to the dreaded sourpuss, Miss A——.

However, I do remember, on the first and last days of nursery school, there being a lot of talk of mothers and their tears.

I had a bit of a cry. It's what we said to each other while pulling mysteriously soppy faces. But I'm still not sure what we were supposed to be crying about.

I wonder if anyone did.

And while I'm on the subject of things that were meant to be enjoyable, carefree mini–rites of passage . . .

3. Snobbery

I met a woman recently, so desperate to get her child into a fashionable nursery school that she had her husband call the school's admissions office from her maternity hospital bed. But there you have it. Some people are silly.

4. School Entrance

We are treated to a constant stream of articles, studies, movies, comedy shows, and vacuous chick-lit novels about the appalling pressures placed on "normal" mothers at school entrances across the land. Mothers, it seems, have a rotten time of it out there. In fact (a recent study revealed . . .), an astonishing 39 percent of all mothers are made to feel like "complete failures" by the other mothers at school. It seems hard to believe. Also, it makes me wonder, Who ever framed such an odious question? And why? Have any of us ever been asked if we felt like "utter failures" at any other of life's relatively ordinary pit stops? At the doctor's office, the cafeteria at work, the bus stop, the gym? I certainly haven't. But I've often been asked about the "hell" of school drop-off. Why is that? Two words: cultural misogyny.

Come the start of each new academic year, women journalists who really ought to know better are wheeled out to whip up the annual mothers hate-fest. "Other mothers" are presented as caricatures of idiocy, snobbery, cut-throat competitiveness, and petty-minded malice: monster women who judge and condemn one another on the strength of their school-run hair and ability to remember packed lunches.

The problem stems, I suppose, from the maternal inadequacy and guilt that bubbles beneath the simpering, smiling surface of us all. Our sense of loserhood has to find an outlet somewhere, so we turn on each other. In the long run it can only feed the loserhood fire.

After all, if a mother turns up with a homemade snack prepared each morning and mascara on, does it mean she's doing a better job at raising her children than I am at raising mine? Does it mean she's a better mother or a better woman? Does it mean she has superior children? These questions don't even merit answers. She's just clever at early morning mascara, managing things her way, trying very hard to raise the sort of child she wants to raise, according to the rules and standards that she considers important.

The temptation to turn this figure into a judgmental scold is hard to resist, but to what end? There is malice wherever humans fester. Significantly less—in my experience—at the school entrance than in a newspaper office.

Thirty-nine percent of all mothers are made to feel like "complete failures" by the other mothers at the school entrance. Really? It's a school entrance, for crying out loud! Peopled by fellow mothers, some brighter and some kinder than others; each one ferreting for air beneath her own invisible shroud of guilt and uncertainty; each one only present because she really loves her child.

5. Supermothers

Still, some mothers are nightmares. Not all Supers are equally awful; some are more awful than others. In the great wash of mothers-at-school-drop-off, they form only a tiny group, but they make more noise than everyone else put together (it's why we can't help but notice them).

In my mind I have a prototype, an amalgamation-concentrate of all the rich, bossy, loud, and pointlessly over-organized mothers I've ever encountered. And they're not monsters. I suppose. They just happen to seriously piss other people off.

The first Supers—for the sake of clarity, let's call them the "Super-Supers"—originated in the United States. The main difference between the American and British variant seems to be that the UK Super doesn't bother with the same level of personal grooming. The implication being (I have always assumed) that for the Brit Mum self-adornment is simply too trivial a task when compared with the vast and vital other responsibilities they face each morning: getting the kids to school earlier than everyone else, their bellies groaning with appropriately healthful breakfasts. I find the British supermothers, with their graceless, English, barking voices, even more depressing than the American version. Puffy and gray-faced, and perma-disapproving, they look like the battle-axes they really are. No Botox or fillers for them. Nothing so frivolous. Just a few token lady accessories tossed onto their bossy frames: valuable earrings, fussy overcoats—always noticeably expensive, always unflattering.

Supermothers arrive ahead of the gaggle for the morning drop-off, sometimes wearing shiny running clothes, always on top of things. They talk loudly and often, I've noticed, incessantly: either to each other, organizing playdates with the urgency of world leaders discussing the withdrawal from Afghanistan, or to their children, issuing instructions in perky ultrareasonable voices. And every morning, it seems, they have something new, earnest, and vital to impart to the children's teacher, so they stand at the entrance to the classroom, necks out like turkeys, blocking the doorway and stopping anybody else from getting in or out.

They book the best slots at parent-teacher conferences, usually before anyone else even knows the date. They send out "save the date" e-mails in advance of their children's birthday party invitations and, if they're not overseas during school holidays—which, thankfully, they generally are—mass e-mails with fun suggestions, often requiring children to be driven to unnecessary places at inconvenient times of the day, to do pointless activities that almost certainly cost money.

They organize expensive, skill-enhancing activities for

their children every weekday after school except—and we really ought to know it, because they've told us a hundred times—the third Tuesday of every month; and for those third Tuesdays they organize "Tuesday playdates" weeks, even months, in advance. They do their children's homework for them if the homework is craft-related, and they strut into school with their 3-D papier-mâché models of Mount Vesuvius like they think they're Damien Hirst.

The fundamental belief of supermother-dom, it seems, is that the world can, and must, be melded to facilitate their child's path through life. And what's so irritating is that these women appear to possess limitless supplies of all the necessary resources—time, money and brute-faced shamelessness—to ensure that they bring that about.

Supers aren't stupid. Or not in the conventional sense. That is, often they are highly educated. Often, pre-children, they had impressive, high-earning careers of their own. And with all the money and energy, all the care, self-discipline, and detailed attention these women pour into the task, it's hardly surprising that they succeed. Supers create a super-breed: superprogeny, good at an awful lot of things. Good at everything, actually, that requires private tuition and concentrated, dedicated adult intercession. Other children, with lazier, busier, and/or more impoverished mothers, cannot hope to compete.

So it is that the self-perpetuation of the Supers continues. They win places to the best schools, and then to the best universities, and then the best jobs at the best banks and the best consultancy firms, and, in due course, they roll home in orderly fashion, with all the best salaries, and the process begins all over again.

The question is, Does it matter? Do we really want our children to join them on their joyless trudge through life's to-do lists? We all want our children to thrive, obviously. But there are a million ways to do that. The Supers, lacking in imagination what they so feverishly make up for in cash and efficiency, only understand one way. Their children will grow up rich and efficient. Twenty years hence, over their Christmas Day or Thanksgiving lunches, with massively ornate and often fairly disgusting vegetable side dishes, they will feel (at least I hope so) reasonably comfortable in one another's company.

But for all the money and effort and micromanagement that's put into their upbringing, there isn't much evidence that the superprogeny, with its advanced trombone, its trophy in interschool trampolining, and its cum laude Ivy League degree in geography, is any more contented than the rest of us. Nor any more beloved. Nor (and this has to count for something) making any more of a contribution to the health, beauty, wisdom, or gaiety of our shared universe.

6. Conversations About Schools

There's a wonderful scene in Luc Besson's 1985 movie *Subway* in which Isabelle Adjani, having sat sullenly through the first half of a bourgeois dinner party, can suddenly endure her neighbor's complacent conversation not a moment longer. "Stop!" she interrupts her. "Tell it to someone else because I don't give a fuck for your bullshit."

I think longingly of that line every time local parents get together and, like clockwork, our conversation turns, so earnest and so respectable, as if our lives depended on it, to the subject of schools: specifically, the pros and cons of different (private) schools in our area. All of which are excellent. Lucky us. None of which, finally, will be the deciding factor in how our children's lives and personalities pan out. This one offers Mandarin! I wasn't terribly impressed by the math curriculum in that one. The other one has superb sporting facilities!

Can we find something else to talk about now? (Just not property prices.)

7. Sniffles, Sickly Children, and Staying Home from School

After many years of working for small, struggling private companies, a friend of mine took a job in the public sector. It turned out to be a pleasant job, and she was reasonably happy. But it required quite a period of adjustment. There was, she said, a fundamental—actually quite a shocking—difference in her new colleagues' approach to work: most noticeably in how healthy they believed they needed to feel before they might be willing to get down to it.

On a Wednesday morning soon after she had started the job, she received an e-mail from a senior colleague who had decided not to come in for the rest of the week. The reason given was:

"I'm not feeling 100 percent. Not even 80 percent actually and I don't want to spread anything around. At this point I think it's better for me to stay home until after the weekend, so I can really knock it on the head."

And as I send in my taxes, I will try my best not to think of the man in his bed, chasing those elusive last few percent.

It may simply be the case that—despite my tightfisted

refusal to buy organic food, or really to fuss about my children's diet at all, except occasionally to say, "Maybe you should eat an apple if there is one, before you finish all those crackers"—my children are (at the time of this writing) blessed with unusually strong constitutions. It might simply be that, in which case I offer thanks to the gods of good health. Or it might be that, in a household where both earners are self-employed, the suggestion that anyone should stay home in bed is a thing to be dreaded—as long as we're functioning at anything above, oh, I don't know (these things are hard to measure), let's say 16 percent?

As long as there's no actual measurable fever, I do not make the prospect sound appealing. "You *can* stay home," I say to the children, slightly impatiently. "If you *really* don't feel up to it. It's up to you. *It's your call.* But you'll be very bored and very lonely. Why don't you sort of go to school and then see how it works out? If you feel absolutely rotten, then we'll find a way of getting you home again."

8. Homework

The point of it, I thought, was for children to practice what they had been taught at school and learn to work on their own. I don't mind being called over to help if a child gets stuck (although Google is often a safer bet), but when they're beyond the age of seven, let's say, I am bewildered by the notion that I might be expected to sit down at the kitchen table with them, night after night, and nurse them through each task and question.

Children are often asked to design posters for their homework. Which is fun. One morning several years ago I was accompanying my child—then about nine years old—with a homework poster to the classroom. She had been quite proud of it when she'd finished it the previous evening, and I, too, had thought it was a masterpiece. But as we drew closer to her homeroom, several of her classmates sauntered by, many of them with beautiful, symmetrical, info-packed, plastic-laminated artwork tucked neatly under their little arms.

I said to my child: Oh my God—have you seen?

By comparison, her poster was crap. There was no denying it. And yet I knew she had tried reasonably hard: I had spotted her out of the corner of my eye, printing and cutting and folding and sticking at the kitchen table, while I was tapping away. Until then I had always assumed she was reasonably competent. But her poster was useless! Was she a dolt after all? Was it possible? The evidence was certainly pointing that way. I felt extremely sad. So sad that I was later moved to ask the teacher.

"Is my girl an idiot?" I asked. "Is she as dozy as her poster seems to imply?"

The teacher said the girl was doing just fine. And advised me to advise my child not to be disheartened. Half of the posters, he said, will have been done by the mothers. "It's always very obvious when the mothers are doing it for them. And obviously it gets reflected in the final mark."

My child was not a sandwich short of a picnic after all! It was just that she had done her homework.

One less thing to worry about. Which isn't to say (I should add, with a small but noticeable clearing of throat) that homework efforts don't need to be policed. And I can see that some children might benefit significantly from a less libertarian approach. Nevertheless—there is a difference between checking a child's homework when it's finished and kicking up a stink if it's useless (boring but possibly essential) and actually sitting down and doing the homework for and with them. (Boring, time-consuming, and counter-productive.)

After all, you can't take your mommy into the exam room, can you? You cannot. And thank goodness for that.

9. Tutors

People lie about their personal tutor habit almost as much as they lie about their sex lives. Like nannies and other domestic helpers, tutors are a sort of dirty secret of the middle class, their existence often blatantly denied by the parents who employ them. I don't know why. Unless, of course, one of the parents is a politician or one of the thousands who claim to take a moral stand against the inequities of private education.

The other thing worth remembering about tutors, by the way, is that some are more cynical than others and that, at seventy-five dollars an hour, their livelihood depends on parents feeling insecure and worried about their children's education. If—as has happened to me—a particular tutor makes a habit of whipping you up into a frenzy of concern, just breathe deep (I forgot to do this) and remember: things may not be half as bad as they say.

Far from it, in fact. Children develop at different rates. And that's okay. Isn't it? I think so.

It's a dirty business, earning a living. And tutors have mortgages, too.

10. Nits

Hedrin. It doesn't stink, and it actually works. But it costs a fortune. With the money I've spent, over the years, on bottles of Hedrin and other less effective lice-attacking treatments, I could probably buy—well, now, definitely a vacation somewhere. Possibly a house in the South of France. In fact, a few years ago, so desperate was I for a lice-and-nit-free household, I forwent the bloody Hedrin and attended, en famille, a special nit-terminating "salon" in a posh part of North London, where an army of nit killers—dressed, oddly, like astronauts—put specially adapted Hoovers to our heads. Sitting with her children at the Hoover beside mine, by the way, was Thandie Newton, Famously Beautiful Movie Star . . . that's correct . . . because it turns out even Famously Beautiful Movie Stars get nits off their children.

Anyway, the point is, no matter what you do, no matter how much money and effort and bloodlust you throw into the eradication project, someone in a classroom somewhere always has nits, and one way or another, lice—like the Terminator, will always "be back." It's an unwinnable battle and there comes a moment when you have to ask yourself, Is it worth the fight?

The first time I encountered lice was before I had children of my own. A young niece or nephew had left a few drowned bodies in the bottom of their grandparents' bathtub one day. I kicked up an almighty fuss. Those little drowned insects—synonymous to me, back then, with dirt and rats and possibly typhoid—struck me, in my dainty child-free state, as the most disgusting things I'd ever encountered.

But familiarity breeds—if not affection, then complacency, at least. Once you've been host to them yourself a couple of times, pulled them out of your children's hair more times than you can count, it's hard to sustain the same sense of outrage when yet another one comes along. Obviously, having a head that's crawling with lice is faintly repellent. Okay, it's completely revolting. Bring on the Hedrin. But the odd one or two, roaming about? They don't do any harm, after all. Like the rest of us, they're only trying to eke out a life for themselves. Poor things. Who are we to begrudge that?

"For there is nothing either good or bad," as Hamlet wisely observed, "but thinking makes it so." I'm pretty sure he was referring to head lice at the time.

11. School Meetings Requiring the Presence of Quietly Smiling Moms

No shortage of these, are there? Sometimes I wonder if they're not piled on in quite the way they are specifically to antagonize busy mothers. Obviously, in principle, the more a school welcomes its parents in, the better. That said . . .

Since, for most of us, attending all these events is impossible, it makes sense, for our own peace of mind, to free ourselves from too strong a sense of obligation about them. It's no fun feeling like you're letting people down. Better to lower expectations (yours and theirs) from the start.

With three children, not all at the same school, I think if I attended everything I was meant to, all the matches, sports days, swimming contests, school parties, concerts, plays, discussions about new high school standards, discussions about the food in the cafeteria, my life might well grind to a halt.

Most of the time, the Lazy Mothering modus as propagated on these pages works for the greater enjoyment of both parties—mother and child—or at least not at the cost of either, but I can't quite pull off the argument here. My children (less as they grow older, of course) would generally prefer it if I attended their school functions. Why wouldn't they? And yet I still don't. Because, as I explain to the children, time is of the essence. Although I love them tenderly (*duh*), there are often other things—not related to them—that I either need or would prefer to be doing.

Added to which, by the way, even if I didn't have work to do; even if I had a fleet of nannies and housekeepers and—gosh—a tax-deductible chauffeur to attend to the parking, I would still want to limit what hours I spent, in this short life, making polite conversation on rain-soaked sidelines or sitting in school halls watching other people's children playing musical instruments badly.

Children who grow up understanding that their mother's world doesn't solely revolve around theirs are much the better for it. In my opinion. That is to say, I think it makes them less self-centered, more self-reliant, and, well, better feminists, three qualities I happen to rate above most. Other mothers lay greater emphasis on different human qualities, and so bring up their children differently. . . .

In any case, my children seem to take it in stride.

In the early years, before it occurred to me what a high proportion of these wretched occasions amounted to nothing much more than Stepford-style exercises in mommy-hoop-jumping, I did indeed try to participate in as many of them as possible: attended after-drop-off, get-to-know-each-other coffee mornings; end-of-year, get-pissed-together summer parties. I have accompanied classes on trips to pantomimes and museums (okay, one pantomime, one museum);

I have sat and sweated by the side at municipal swimming pools, whooping encouragement while my children doggy-paddled from one shallow end to another. I have sold second-hand clothes at the school fair, and cakes at the cake stand, and books at the book stand, and so on.

I certainly wouldn't pretend to have done my bit: nor anywhere near. Not compared to the extraordinary efforts put in by some of the mothers. Nevertheless, I have done *a* bit. Some of it was good fun. Some of it was useful. Most of it was painless enough. But all of it eats up precious time.

What infuriates me are those occasions where you *know* your presence is unnecessary and improves nothing for anyone—and yet still you attend, for the solitary reason that you "feel you must"; because everyone else is. Because they felt they must, too.

But why?

Because our children want us there.

But why do our children want us there?

Because . . . their friends' mothers are there.

But why are their friends' mothers there?

Because. Just because. You know?

We're all there on the whims of our precious children, but nobody really knows why.

I attended a welcome-to-autumn-term meeting at one or other school or nursery school, many years ago, that ground to a halt when one of the mothers wondered how the children could be encouraged to wash their hands before and after using the water fountain. So we sat on our minuscule chairs: a room full of intelligent, busy, educated women, many of whom had left work specifically to be present, while a discussion slowly unfolded and slowly went nowhere at all, about the germs that might possibly lurk near water fountains in muddy playgrounds. Nobody said:

Come on, guys, this is a non-problem. Can we move on? Nobody said it. We simply sat there, politely smiling. Just because. That's what the other mothers did. Because that's what mothers do.

I attended another meeting in another school assembly hall, this one about the possibility of children embarking on a weeklong cultural exchange with some students in China, of all magnificent adventures. I sat in that school hall for an hour, tick-tock, tick-tock, while the neurotic faction tossed in their degenerate questions:

"What if the kids don't like the Chinese food?"

"Will the host school be providing a Western-style menu option?"

But I digress. (Only—it is staggering what some people will find to worry about, and how shameless they are about airing it; and how feeble the rest of us are, allowing them to do it on our time.)

The point is, there are many aspects to family life, and I don't think it's too controversial to suggest that different mothers lay emphasis on and draw pleasure from different aspects. Some mothers genuinely enjoy going to meetings. I don't. Some mothers genuinely believe that playground hygiene around the water fountain is a valid and interesting preoccupation: something that's worth dedicating an afternoon to discussing. And although I will never understand why, I certainly don't want to prevent them from indulging that innocent pleasure. Only, please, don't make it something the rest feel obliged to listen in on.

12. After-School Activities, School Holidays, and Day Camps

My heart used to sink when I returned home to find the children flopped in front of the Wii—or in front of any screen, come to think of it. (Weekends don't count.) Life is so short, I would think frantically, and it's not even raining outside! They should be *doing* something, learning something, being stimulated, acquiring skills! And yet here they are, cooped up in an overheated living room, possibly without having bothered to switch the lights on, the haze of inertia so thick around them it almost gleams. . . .

Of all the aspects of child rearing, it's the one that, in the early years, tormented me most: the tidal wave of guilt that hit me each time I returned from work to see my children looking listless and bored, as well as each time one of the supermothers sent one of their ridiculous round-robins, suggesting yet more Day Camps, Fun Days, or after-school clubs—every one of which cost money, every one of which required transportation to and from.

Children have so much free time. The school holidays are so long. We can't provide them with entertainment each and every day; practically and financially (for me, at least), it is an impossibility. What are we to do with them?

That was one of the reasons the family moved out of the city, however briefly. The guilt, oh, the guilt! I fondly imagined, with all those fields outside, that the problem of Amusing the Children, in a wholesome and possibly even educational manner, would be cheaply and easily resolved. I listened to the propaganda that dribbled from the mouths of the evacuees, those former urbanites who had decamped to the country before us (most of whom, I've since discovered, spend their waking hours behind the wheel of a car, driving children to school and back and parties and back and trampoline clubs and tap dance classes . . .). "Oh, we just open the back door," they said smugly, "and we toss the kids outside and we don't see them again until teatime." Stupidly (bearing in mind that I grew up in the country myself) or, perhaps, out of sheer, blind desperation, I believed them.

I remember, a month or two after we had moved to the country, urging my daughter, then seven, to switch off the TV and go outside and play. She said, "Trouble is, though, it turns out fields are quite boring."

I had fields galore where I grew up. And they weren't always boring. But they often were. For my generation, boredom, as I said, was part of life.

And maybe it's because childish boredom can be so easily and immediately resolved now—just toss them in front of a screen and you won't hear from them again until teatime or tomorrow or next year—that we tend to feel so uncomfortable with it.

In any case, country life didn't solve anything. Same screens. Same inertia.

We returned to London, and the question of how-to-amuse-the-children remained as desperate as ever. The situation was soon out of control. Between them, they were attending trampoline camps and drama lessons, football coaching and hip-hop dance classes, modern dance, ballet, swimming classes, and stand-up comedy lessons (I exaggerate not), and though, in truth, it was remarkably little compared with the after-school activities of many of their friends, it was more than I could afford. Until finally, thankfully, came one too many extracurricular extravagances; that one broke the camel's back, which gave me the courage to dump the lot of them. (Well, most.)

13. Watching Children Enjoying Hobbies

Like a lot of boys, my son loves soccer. I am proud of his dedication and skill and delighted by his passion. My younger daughter, meanwhile, loves coloring, baking inedible "cakes," and bouncing on trampolines. My older daughter enjoys all sorts of things: among them, writing plays and playing tennis and making subtly delicious toasted sandwiches. All this is good.

Having hobbies is good. But I don't think they need endless parental validation before they can be considered a pleasure. Parents don't need to stand by and watch. Far better, I would have thought, that they get a life and find some hobbies of their own.

If a child develops a passion for pottery, let's say, there may sometimes be a nice pot to be rejoiced over along the way. And an enthusiastic mother, on spotting excellent pottery promise in her offspring, might take care to provide said offspring with, I don't know, access to a kiln. But is she also required to sit around, life on hold, and watch while the child models the clay? I think not. By the same token, nor do I feel duty-bound to watch my children playing their weekly sports matches, any more than I would expect even the most ardent of admirers to watch and applaud, in the cold and the rain, while I sat reading a magazine.

Sport is not a performance art. Lots of people enjoy watching it—yes (not me)—but that's not its raison d'être. Its raison d'être is in the taking part.

It's a symptom of our neurotic meddlesomeness—the overinflated belief in our own importance as parents, and a lack of faith in our children's ability to enjoy life independent of our active approval—that sends us out there to the sidelines, week after ice-cold week, to watch and clap and shout while our child . . . has fun. Why bother? Why not find our own fun? Our children will have plenty enough fun without us standing there; possibly (dare I suggest?) without us breathing down their necks, they might even have more.

14. Fund-Raising

If you're feeling really brave (count me out on this one), you might want to throw in a question about what fund the cake is being baked to raise money for. It's one thing, raising money for charity. It's another thing (and this—especially, but not exclusively—applies to private schools) that we should busy ourselves raising money for an educational establishment that already has enough to be getting on with.

It's as if school fund-raising were a nervous tick: just something extra for mothers and fathers to fuss about, like tidying and retidying your desk before finally getting down to work. I'm treading on shaky ground here; I am not a teacher. What do I know about which extravagant gadgets and pieces of equipment are actually worthwhile teaching aids? Nothing much. But I remember this:

When I was a child, the principal at my village elementary school waged a long campaign for the entire school to be relocated in a brand-new building up the road. (She got it in the end. The old school building, last I checked, is a desirable house belonging to a local doctor.) Anyway, I was lolling by the school gate one day, waiting for my mother to pick me up, listening in on two other mothers discussing the building campaign.

"It's disgusting," the smaller one said, and the other one, very tall, with blotchy skin, nodded so hard her cheeks wobbled. "In this day and age," the little one said, "it's a disgrace that the kiddies have to cross the playground to get to the toilets. In the rain and the snow . . ."

"In this day and age," repeated the tall one. "It's disgusting."

I remember gazing from one to the other, wondering what they were fussing about. What was so "disgusting" about crossing the playground? I didn't mind. It hadn't occurred to me to mind. It was just something you did if you wanted to get to the bathroom.

God knows how many busy-mom fund-raisers (and how much taxpayers' money) later, the will of the principal finally prevailed. We had a spanking-new building, and we didn't have to cross the playground to go to the bathroom anymore. And, by the way, that was a shame. Because as a child, it's quite fun to cross the playground from time to time.

Schools—private and public—seem to get a bit hung up on student comfort and equipment—and honestly, I can't be the *only* parent who doesn't care, who positively prefers it, actually, if the children sometimes have to "mend and make do" (as they said in the olden days). Necessity is the mother of invention and all that. As long as a school has the essentials—intelligent, kind, imaginative teachers, and enough space and whatever else constitutes the "essentials." If I were ever going to bake a cake for a fund-raiser (which is unlikely), it would need to be for a decent cause: a local hospice, let's say. Something valid. And not so my precious kiddies could have a machine for pitching baseballs. And certainly not so they could enjoy uninterrupted central heating en route to the bathroom.

15. Distressing Cakes

It's the opening scene of a successful novel. Isn't it? At any rate, it's the opening scene in the film of the book, which I couldn't watch beyond the first fifteen minutes because I simply couldn't understand the silly woman's problem. What was she meant to be achieving by beating up store-bought cakes so that they would look homemade? And why were we supposed to sympathize with her? In her desperation to conform to a set of rules she clearly didn't believe in, she only perpetuated what, it seems to me, has always been an odious and unhelpful pretense: that good mothers should feel obliged to make time for baking (a pastime that has become symbolic of all the old-fashioned maternal virtues).

Aside from exhausting herself for no sensible reason, the "heroine," coward that she is, was passing on a message to her child that it's better to cower and pretend, to do as you're told, no matter how preposterous, than to speak up for yourself and refuse to be pushed around.

Seriously, though. If we can't say no for ourselves, we might do it for our daughters: save them from being led to the same ridiculous dance twenty-five years down the road.

Next time a letter comes home asking for a cake for the cake sale, simply explain (what they all know perfectly well anyway) that you won't because

You

Don't

Have

Time.

And because the store-bought cakes taste better anyway.

Part V

Charm School

1. Good Manners and Charm

Are more or less the same thing and, in a civilized world, after an ability to lie, are possibly the most vital of all the life skills. As I tell my children: properly applied, they can ease the path to the moon.

So it's peculiar that, often, the most intensely tended children, with the most perfectionist, most persnickety mothers, are least aware of this basic but essential truth.

I have lost count of the number of visiting children who, when their parents arrive to take them home (see above and, indeed, below), sweep out of the house without pausing to say thank you. It *really* pisses me off. Lesson 1 in Basic Charm Skills only requires two things: to say please, to say thank you, and—okay, three things—to make eye contact, even if it's only for a split second at the moment of uttering the words.

The child's parent knows to say thank you and says it on the child's behalf. Sometimes the parent might even make a halfhearted attempt to prompt the child into saying it for themselves: *"Have you got your shoes? Shall we zip up your coat? Did you have a good time? Are you going to say thank you?*" But when the children, inexplicably (because after all, why not?), refuse to oblige, or when they mumble the words in hostile fashion while gazing at the floor—their parents don't pursue it. They roll their eyes. Shrug. Ruffle their horrible little child's hair. *Hey-ho. Kids will be kids!*

And I smile politely, tussling silently with my inner demon as it urges me to reach for the nearest bat and whack the pair of them over the head.

2. Swearing

I was walking along the street with my two-and-a-half-year-old son, many moons ago, and we bumped into a neighbor. The neighbor and I stopped to chat, which, as any child would tell you, was annoying. My son tugged on my arm and waited impatiently for the conversation to finish. Finally the neighbor bent down to address him.

"Hello there, little fellow!" he said, in conventional, booming, child-friendly tones. "How are we today? Are we off to the shop with Mommy then?"

And why, yes! Indeed, so we were! It wasn't a difficult question. I had every confidence my son could deal with it himself. So I said nothing and only prepared to wallow and bask in the inevitable cuteness of his reply. But it didn't come. To my dismay, he said nothing at all. Instead, he gave a small, fey whimper and hid behind my leg.

"Is Mommy going to buy you some candy?" the neighbor persevered. "I expect you'd like that! Wouldn't that be great?"

And why, yes, indeed, it would have been great! But the

boy still uttered nothing, not a word. Just another sad, bored whimper, teetering on a fully fledged wail.

The neighbor soon lost interest. I apologized for my goofy little son, and the lad and I continued on our journey.

"What happened there?" I asked him, when we were out of earshot. "Why didn't you answer the neighbor?"

He shrugged.

"Have you forgotten what you're meant to say to grown-ups when they say hello to you? What are you supposed to say?"

He replied: "I'm supposed to say 'hello.'"

"Exactly!" I cried triumphantly. "That's exactly right! And what *aren't* you supposed to do? When a grown-up tries to make conversation with you?" The correct answer to which, clearly, was "Cling to my mother's leg and whimper."

He thought about it.

"I'm pretty sure you know the answer," I kept on. "What *don't* you do when a grown-up tries to make conversation with you?"

"I think," he said finally, "I don't say '*fuck*.'"

It was a golden moment for me, a moment of intense maternal pride.

Close students of this important text may already have noticed that its author swears quite a lot. There are times, I find, when only a swear word will satisfy. Besides, I read somewhere (recent studies have shown) that the act of swearing releases chemicals into the blood—or possibly the brain?—that have a soothing effect on the body, similar to painkillers. Or was it tranquilizers? Or maybe it was laughing gas? In any case, I swear because it pleases, because I know it teases, and because some of the best curses have a magnificently punchy ring to them when used with sufficient chutzpah; and it does the heart good, from time to time, to get one's lips (and keyboard) around them. I swear in front of the children, always have and always will. Partly, as an admittedly infantile but strangely satisfying rebellion against the oppressive gods of propriety and tastefulness that rule the world of nicey-nicey parenting. I say *partly,* but now that I think about it, that may be the only reason. Or the main reason.

I never did much alter my vocabulary for the children, nor any other aspect of the way I communicate. I'm not sure that it ever even occurred to me. My parents didn't do it for us. They never patronized us. Never used special kiddie-friendly words or voices. They always talked, often swore, and assumed that at some point, if we were sufficiently interested, we would catch on. And it was good. Excellent, even. It kept us on our toes. In this, it has always felt natural to do the same. Long words, complicated ideas, and uncomfortable subject matter—peppered with curse words where necessary—have generally been the order of every day.

Because things are there to be learned, are they not? Everything is there to be learned and, once learned, to be exploited intelligently.

My two-and-a-half-year-old son understood the rules of engagement. Bless his goofy socks. Knowing stuff is good; knowing when and where (not) to apply the knowledge is even better. Don't say "fuck" to people who will find it shocking. But own that word, and understand—if you find yourself short of laughing gas—that it's sometimes a useful one to call upon.

3. Sexualization of Children

Children look preposterous when they strut about in adult clothing, copying the dance moves they've watched on TV. Then again, the stars themselves, adult women in often quite silly clothes, mouthing meaningless words, grinding their hips into thin air and gazing longingly at us all, look more than a little preposterous, too. At least when children mimic them, they tend to realize it's funny.

Additionally, there is the other, less comfortable point, which in our ever-more-puritanical and sentimental approach to childhood, we are prone to overlook: most children are never wholly unsexual. I could provide a long, embarrassing list of people I had crushes on from about the age of seven years old. It starts with little Mark Lester, of *Oliver!* fame, with whom I was truly infatuated. And it includes the Bionic Woman.

Maybe it's a natural response to the guilt and confusion we feel for our sexualized modern world, but as adults we tend, increasingly, to exaggerate not just the sexual purity of our children, but the value of that purity, too.

A friend of mine was taken aside by his eight-year-old daughter's teacher because one child had reported to her mother, who had lodged a complaint with the school, that he had used "sexual language inappropriately, referring to the sex act" in the child's presence.

He'd hit his thumb hammering a nail into the kitchen wall while she was present at a playdate with his daughter, and he'd shouted, "Fuck!" Which I call a fairly moderate response. Now when he goes to pick up his daughter, he walks around the school with an imaginary sign hanging round his neck, if he can bring himself to visit the school at all.

I am amazed, often, by parents' knee-jerk prissiness when it comes to their children's exposure to any aspect of sex. It is part of who we are; it's one of the better aspects (can be) of being human. And maybe, if we weren't so squeamish about it, modern sexual appetites wouldn't be quite so dependent on hyperreal body shapes and screen-delivered pantomime-sex shows for fulfillment.

4. Lying

How lovely to see you!
I love my job.
I love your mother.
I love you.
That was delicious.

I voted Green.
I called, but I think your mobile must have been off.
I can't afford it.
I can afford it.
I remember it well.
It was on sale.
I haven't got any change.

Sorry, I'm busy that night.
Luckily I'm not busy that night.
I don't really smoke.
I wish I could, but I can't.

You look lovely.
Your children are adorable.
We'd love to come.
What a beautiful service!
Honestly, I really don't mind.

Horrible traffic.
I assumed you knew.
The e-mail must have gone astray.
There wasn't any reception.
We're putting everything we have behind it.
I'm in a meeting.
That took me *hours*.

He's in a meeting.
I'm sick in bed.
I cooked it myself.
He's sick in bed.
I can't hear you—you're breaking up.
There's someone at the door.
My alarm didn't go off.
Of course I was in.
I'm on my way.
I left half an hour ago.
Only two glasses, Officer.
I completely forgot!
It came out of the blue.
I did not inhale.

It's going really well.

Nothing is the matter.

No.

Yes.

We've almost completely sold out.

It wasn't my fault.

I wish I could help you.

It's not company policy.

I'm so excited.

I'm sorry, it's just not possible.

That's my highest offer.

He started it.

No, I don't think you're stupid.

I've already checked.

Yes, I'm certain.

I had no idea.

That's a lie!

I have to rush.

We'll be sad to lose you.

I haven't breathed a word.

There's nothing more I can do.

I've never had Botox.

I don't believe in diets.

I loved that book.

I definitely locked the door.

I do understand.

You had it last.

You're not fat.
I am listening.

You were brilliant.
I was offended.
I wasn't offended.
That's not funny.
That is funny.
I'm definitely not giving up.
How interesting.

We never have sex anymore.
We have sex all the time.
That was fantastic.
I did not have sexual intercourse with that woman.

It's peculiar, isn't it, how adults take such a ferociously dim view of their children lying when we spend so much time lying ourselves. We lie and are lied to so much, we hardly bother to notice it. In fact, lying is the cement that holds our ludicrous adult world together. And I don't mean what, in our mealymouthed way, we call "white" lies—I mean lies of every hue and every color. We would be lost without them.

So it seems to me that the sooner children learn how to lie efficiently, the better their chances of survival in this dishonest world.

I wonder if parents hate to be lied to not because lying is wrong (we're on shaky ground) but because the moment a child lies, he reclaims a little of his birthright, his power as a separate individual. A lying child crosses what was always an unsustainable "boundary" and steps into a lawless world of her own creation, of which she is master and over which a parent can have no control.

I don't like it when my children lie to me, obviously. It makes me feel ostracized and it makes me worry about what they may be trying to hide. On the other hand, I have to acknowledge that it takes a certain gumption to do it—a refusal to kowtow to my authority. It demonstrates a drive toward self-ownership, independence, and personal survival, which, whether we like it or not, are all vital ingredients for a successful adulthood. And even if lying ought not to be a skill to be overtly applauded (because, of course, in a perfect world we would all tell each other how fat we looked in those trousers, how disgusting our cooking is, and exactly who we screwed, how, where, and when), the act of lying—separate from whatever is being lied about—isn't something to be entirely discouraged.

5. To Lie or Not to Lie?

Whereas I expect to lie to other adults, almost as a matter of course; and whereas I expect other adults to lie to me, also as a matter of course; and whereas I also expect to be lied to by my children, I try on the whole to avoid lying to them. Partly because if they can't trust their mother not to feed them bullshit, who the hell can they trust in this bullshit-sodden world? Partly because it seems to be counterproductive. I want my children to be the smartest they can be.

6. Santa Claus

Consistency, like honesty, can be overrated. Some things are worth lying about.

He's more often referred to as Santa on TV. To me, the name "Santa" conjures everything that is most disheartening about the season: fat, smirking pedophiles with blusher on. Coca-Cola ads.

Santa Claus, on the other hand, seems like a good sort.

However, there is *only one* Santa Claus. He or she shows up just once a year, sometime after midnight, pissed and bumping into things. All the others—most especially those that require parents to stand in line in shopping centers where there is no natural light source—are slightly creepy, intensely depressing, and should climb back into their sleighs and Jingle Bells back to hell.

7. Picking Up Children After "Playdates"

The doorbell rings. You go to answer it and as you do so, you shout up the stairs or along the hallway to the visiting child: "Your mom is here to fetch you" (thereby saving yourself from having to remember which child it is, exactly, who is visiting). The child, who isn't desperate to leave, either ignores you entirely or interprets your call as an amusing cue to venture deeper and/or higher into the house, as far as possible from the front door and the collecting parent. The child and his teatime host (my child) may even—may often—choose to take the hilarious "I'm not going home" jape further still and hide in a closet somewhere, where I think they genuinely believe they will never be found.

So it goes. Children will be children. It wouldn't matter in the least, if only the adults involved could pull together to facilitate a smooth, good-natured, and (above all) brisk extraction of child guest, thereby enabling us all to get on with our lives.

But it never happens. Standing in the hallway, we adults are trapped within our tornado of parental niceties, unable to pause the small talk and yell at the children (though we know they will never emerge without our concentrated insistence) for fear of seeming impatient to get away from each other. Upstairs the children giggle and snort and ransack the closet; downstairs the minutes tick by with neither party certain how, politely, to draw the situation to its mutually longed-for conclusion.

Yes, I was pleased they put swimming back to Fridays again.

They seemed to enjoy their visit to the museum, didn't they?

I hear poor Frankie got a bit carsick on the bus?

He did! But he's fine now. Thank goodness.

Oh! Well. That's all right then.

Are you going away this summer?

It's an impossible situation for both parties. Though there are always exceptions—the odd, full-throttle crazy whose solitary mission, it seems, is to set up camp in your hallway and to never, ever go away—most parents don't *want* to linger in each other's doorways with no definite end in sight, killing themselves softly with politesse.

What we need, I feel, are some guidelines. So here goes:

Picking Up "Playdates": Code of Conduct

1. Picking-up parents, arriving to extract a visiting child, should brief the child in advance of the great event. Preferably in quite a scary way, so that the child definitely absorbs the instruction. A picking-up parent might want to say something along the lines of:

If you leave me stranded in that hallway making small talk with so-and-so's parent while you fart around upstairs hiding in the closet, I swear that I will never, never come and pick you up from anyone's house, ever again.

This might work. But it generally doesn't. In which case, further tactics might need to be considered:

2. A picking-up parent might consider bringing other children with them to sit in the car, thereby providing a reasonable excuse to move things along in an urgent manner without offending the host.

3. Picking-up parents who bring younger children with them to the door should *hold on to them tight,* never allowing them to venture any deeper into the house than where the host parent is standing (usually a few feet in front of the door, trying to obstruct the route).

4. If the picking-up parent has not been offered a drink in, let's say, the first six and a half minutes, it's probably an indication that the host parent needs to get on with his or her day. This means that if they then offer you a drink in the seventh minute, they're doing it on sufferance, out of sheer desperation, and under no circumstances should you accept it. Take the invitation in the spirit in which it was meant: fetch your child and get the hell out of the hallway.

5. Can we all agree that it's okay to yell at children hiding in closets? Host parents may look embarrassed. They

may even look disapproving. But underneath, they'll be celebrating.

6.   Parents picking up children in cities or in other places where traffic cops are known to lurk can always pretend they have left the car illegally parked. This allows them to be really very assertive about the extraction, possibly (although this can be awkward) by venturing into the upstairs closet to scoop the wretched child out for themselves.

7.   If the visiting child, having finally emerged from the closet, announces that it now can't find its backpack/ sweater, it is perfectly reasonable, not to say essential, after a token mini-search for said possessions, for the picking-up parent to take the child home regardless, with a request that the host child bring whatever is missing to school the following morning.

8.   And that's it. I won't mention the thing about that final moment, when the picking-up parent really ought to ensure that the visiting child looks their host in the eye and says thank you. Because I've already made the point.

9.   But they should.

8. Saying "Playdate"

It's not pretty, is it? We don't say "sexdate," "watching-amoviedate," "drinkingalcoholdate." It is simultaneously formal and coy, on a par with "sleepover." And we all march in lockstep with this linguistic orthodoxy. I am vaguely disappointed with myself for having succumbed to either word. But I have, for the time being. You have to pick your battles.

9. Sleepovers

Part of family life, and not necessarily the best part, or not for adult members. Younger children tend to be too excited ever to go to sleep, which can be a nuisance. Also they take over the TV. And they thud about all night and make the house shake and make you worry about what you would do if it actually fell down.

Added to which, very occasionally sleepovers just go wrong: children have meltdowns and parents have to be called to retrieve them in the middle of the night. I've once been called, which is a bore, and I've once had to make the call, which is worse than a bore; it's really, acutely embarrassing: "Hello here. Sorry to bother you, *everything's fine!* It's just that—your child is inconsolably miserable at our house and is begging for you to come and take him home."

On the whole, sleepovers make our children happy. And that makes us happy. Also, it's lovely to get to know our children's friends. But can I just say . . .

Sleepovers do not have to involve freshly laundered sheets or comforters. Children don't care about those sorts of niceties, so why should we? All they need is a sleeping bag, a mattress, if there's one available, or, failing that, sofa cushions, or, failing that, the carpet. At a stretch, I'm willing to provide junior guests with clean pillowcases. But not if I can get away without them.

It seems to me a perfectly reasonable quid pro quo: when guests have reached an age when they want to behave like stuffy adults—to sit with us over dinner discussing interest rates (let's say)—then I'll be more than happy to treat them like stuffy adults: mattress, bed, fresh sheets—the works. Until then, they can take over the TV. They can scatter popcorn all over the house—and polystyrene balls from their broken beanbags. They can stay up until four, painting their nails and/or playing FIFA 13—and emerge from their rooms at noon in search of breakfast. All this they can do. So long as it doesn't keep me awake. And so long as the house doesn't actually fall down. And so long as they attempt to clean up at least most of the mess afterward.

With adult luxuries come adult responsibilities. Whatever excuse it takes. I'm just saying the children's friends are always welcome. They can stay as often as they like. But I definitely can't be bothered to make them up a bed.

10. Dressing for the Weather

It's another theme that looms large in the hallways of the Northern Hemisphere, often played out at tedious length by picking-up parents retrieving their children post-"playdate."

Parents expend vast quantities of energy battling with their children to put on coats they don't want to put on. Or battling with them to do up coats they don't want to do up. Or to pile on hats and scarves and gloves when they don't want to pile them on. Two things always strike me about this: the saintliness and patience of the parents and the extreme pointlessness of the exercise.

As often as not, the children are taking only eight short but breezy steps from hallway to the back of a heated car, in any case. It wouldn't matter much, even in a snowstorm, if they made the journey in their underpants. In the olden days, perhaps; before closed-top cars and the invention of penicillin, I can see it made sense to have a more watchful approach to the elements. But these days?

Rather than spending long, dreary moments arguing with children about how hot or cold they might be in the future, it seems more sensible to let them find out for themselves. They have been fitted with their own thermostats, after all.

If they feel cold, they will almost certainly put on a coat.

And if they feel hot, why, they will probably want to take it off again.

And if they leave the house without taking a coat, and then find themselves feeling chilly . . .

(Drumroll, please.)

They'll probably choose to take a coat with them next time!

I dislike telling my children what to do, and avoid it wherever possible. It irritates them, it forces both parties into antagonistic positions and forces out of kilter what is meant to be the underlying music of family life or, at any rate, for me: namely, pleasure in one another's company.

If a child wants to experiment with T-shirts in January, might as well let them. Chances are, they won't want to experiment for very long.

11. Chauffeuring and Public Transportation

Children don't get to roam around much anymore. They tend to be ferried from temperature-controlled inside space to designated sports field and back and forth and back again, without being exposed to much of the world in between. Judging by their drab expressions as they gaze out of their mother's automobile windows, it's every bit as boring for them as we might imagine. Presumably it's pretty boring for their mothers, too.

I live in a comfortable middle-class suburb, full of comfortable middle-class schools. Come eight fifteen on a weekday morning, the roads around me are chockablock with mothers, perched high in impregnable vehicles that were built to withstand the hazards of Alaskan tundra and land mines in Afghanistan, but are used to trundle safely along the dewy London tarmac, between school and soccer and private tutor and piano lesson. I stare at the women's faces, flat with ennui, most of them. And I stare at their children, lolling meekly in the backseats: strapped in, vacant, silent.

What a waste of living time! If the mothers told their

children to climb out of their air-conditioned safety boxes and get on the frigging bus (assuming they live in places where buses and trains are an option)—why! Those women could spend the traffic jam hours, not strumming the steering wheel to FM radio, but fine-tuning their Portuguese! Raising money for dolphins! Painting a modern masterpiece! And their inert-looking children would feel the wind on their cheeks, interact with the world, and it might wake them up a bit.

Nothing, I suppose, could ever be as orderly and secure as a childhood spent strapped into the backseat of an air-conditioned four-wheel drive. And if her child's safety is a mother's single and solitary goal (though it raises the question, *What's the point of giving a person a life if the person's never allowed to live it?*), then I suppose, why yes, what better way to kill the long hours between breakfast and parent-oholic o'clock than in a nice, slow-moving traffic jam?

12. Kiddie Safety Kit

I don't like writing this. It feels like I'm tempting fate.

Terrible things happen. Children get kidnapped and run over and injured and mugged and stabbed and—

STOP.

As children, growing up in the country, my cousin and I used to ride horses a lot. My mother and aunt, who lived side by side, insisted that we wear riding hats—and in fact I think at some point during my youth the wearing of hats might even have become required by law. Or maybe our mothers only told us that because they thought it might encourage us to keep the wretched things on.

But the trouble with hats is that they make your head itch. So we used to put them on as we rode past the house just in case either mother was looking out, and then, as soon as we were out of sight, we took them off and hid them under a tree.

Because it's hard to beat the feeling of total exhilaration—that wild sense of being alive—traveling full pelt, slightly out of control, slightly frightened, with the wind blowing in your hair. To this day those childhood rides over the hills remain among my happiest, most thrilling memories.

There's a nursery school close to where I live today. Its pupils often travel from their mothers' tanks, up the longish garden path to the nursery school door via miniature scooters, handed to them by their solicitous mothers, from the trunks of their megacars; and I notice, more and more, that the majority of the children are only allowed to scoot that safe little journey after their mothers have jammed a great big helmet onto their heads, fastened it tight, and buckled a chin protector under their chins.

Mothers fear for their children. We always have and always will. But our natural aversion to risk—fed, as it is, by the manufacturers of increasingly preposterous "safety products"; fed, too, by the fearmongering in newspapers and on television; fed by ourselves and by each other—seems to me to be teetering on madness. We can never render our children's world 100 percent safe and secure; not without sucking out every ounce of mystery and magic. Protecting our children to the nth degree isn't good parenting. Not really. I don't think so. I think it's selfish parenting.

How and when do we let go? Hell, I don't know! Each to our own. Only it seems sometimes, in our increasingly neurotic need to make everything orderly and perfect for our children, to make no mistakes, to put not a foot wrong and to keep all and any risk at bay, that we forget to introduce them (and ourselves) to the pleasures of simply *living*—not even dangerously: but just living at all.

13. Sports Equipment (Lost and Found)

Sports teachers seem to think parents have a bottomless pit of cash, that we trudge from our breakfast tables to our desks each morning specifically and exclusively so we can earn the money to spend it on variously emblemed, subtly different soccer shirts and hockey fleeces. It's infuriating, but since sports teachers seem to love nothing more than handing out punishments to students who turn up without the correct emblem on the *correct sock,* there's not much to be done about it, except to cough up and buy the wretched stuff. Work a bit harder. Eat a little less. Sell the car. Switch off the central heating. Sell a kidney. I've made the point.

At the start of each year—all right, maybe at the start of every other year; certainly at the start of a new school—I make every effort to outfit the children with (almost) everything on the equipment list. And if, by some fluke, they've managed to hold on to a particular item long enough to grow out of it (ha ha), then it seems unreasonable not to buy them a replacement, at some point.

Beyond that, they're pretty much on their own.

Children can't help losing equipment. A bit like pens. Ballpoint pens come and go. They do the rounds, disappear into a friend's pocket, and then into another friend's pocket, only to reappear in your own pocket—as if by magic—a month or so later. The system works as long as everybody contributes a pen to the cycle every now and then.

Sensible children (and more pragmatic parents) have long since worked out a similar system with sports equipment.

Of course, there will always be other parents, those who want to keep track of their poor children's incomplete equipment, as if it mattered, whip themselves up into a froth by sending out frantic e-mails to class parents, asking us to check equipment bags for their children's missing equipment. It's certainly one way of approaching the problem.

The other is to remain aloof. Where there is a school full of children, there will always be plenty of lost equipment floating around. And so long as we (parents) have, at some point, contributed equivalent equipment to the Lost Property Mountain, it seems perfectly reasonable for our offspring to borrow from that mountain as the need arises. It's an elegant system of communism and recycling, one that I think many parents support, if only tacitly. Everyone saves money, thanks to the array of clothes sizes always available in said mountain. It means children don't have to have nervous breakdowns each time they lose an item of clothing, sports teachers never need to find out, and, just for once, parents don't need to get their wallets out.

Is my daughter wearing somebody else's sweatshirt? Almost certainly. Is somebody else using her tennis racket? Without a doubt. The good news is, it doesn't matter.

I think I've fallen out with one of my oldest friends. His son is my godson, and I forgot his birthday, which misdemeanor, by the way, I do not count as serious. If it counts as a misdemeanor at all. In any case, I was away at the time of the (alleged) offense; his mother and I hadn't been in touch for many months, and the date, never that deeply imprinted, completely slipped my mind. I received a text from the child's mother—no words, no message; just a photograph of the hapless godson, holding a birthday balloon.

It's an honor to be asked to be a godparent, of course. It's wonderful to think that, in years to come, I might be able to help out said friend's child in a way that his parents perhaps cannot. But I think I made a mistake in the early days, when I accepted the role. I should have made it clear: godparenting means different things to different people.

To me, it means:

I'll give him pocket money when I see him. I may even (unlikely, unless I make a fortune; I have children of my own) leave him some cash in my will. I might send him a present via his mother every now and then. If he ever needs a place to sleep, a friendly ear, some introductions in the working world: yup—I'm here to serve. And, may I add, with pleasure. I look forward to knowing him better in the years to come.

But when a relationship becomes nothing but an inflexible checklist of chores, formalities, and to-dos:

> I send a present on this day.
> You send a thank-you letter on that . . .

. . . it's not a relationship, it's a pointless, joyless, grinding bore.

15. Thank-You Letters

I wrote a newspaper article a while back in which I suggested that children should no longer be made to write thank-you letters. Remembering how much I hated to write the stupid things myself, and what a doubly bitter blow it was to receive a worthless present, knowing you would later be required to drum up pen, paper, and gushing enthusiasm, no matter what—I observed that thank-you letters from children had always struck me less as a mark of youthful good manners and more as an adult exercise in (a) competitive mothering (see how quickly my well-trained child writes to you) and (b) revenge:

I have inconvenienced myself by buying and wrapping this present for you. In return, no matter how little you like the present and, in fact, how little time I spent choosing it for you, you must inconvenience yourself by writing to tell me how much you adore it.

The process runs counter to the true spirit of giving.

Added to which, knowing (as we all must) what agonies any child is likely to have suffered in the writing of the wretched thing, it becomes quite hard to read these letters without a lingering sense of shame at having played any part in their suffering.

Thank-you letters are hell to write, often very dull to read, and, above all, a nightmare to bully your children into writing.

In any case, the article provoked an extraordinarily angry response. You might have imagined I had denied the Holocaust. In fact, I received so many outraged e-mails that after a few days, any correspondence with subject headline words including "thank you," "letter," "angry and disappointed," or "people like you don't deserve to have children" were magically filtered directly into my junk folder.

Of course, people who go to the effort of writing very angry letters to newspapers are already a self-defining group: in a carefree moment we might refer to them as "underoccupied lunatics." Nevertheless, loonies though they may be, it takes specific hot topics to bring them out of the woodwork; and "children's thank-you letters," it transpires, pushes all the buttons. Any political party wanting to get elected might bear in mind that they really only need to make two promises:

1. Not to move the clocks back in winter; and

2. To place "thank-you-letter writing skills" on the national curriculum.

16. Squabbling Children

A friend of mine spent a long winter weekend alone with her two sons a few years ago. The little boys squabbled incessantly. Sometimes, for hours at a time, you can simply tune out and leave them to it. Get off—you didn't—I did—Ow!—give me that—fuck off—

(Don't swear.)

He started it—I started it—You started it. That's a lie. I thought of it—give me that—fuck off—

(Don't swear.)

Ow!

We can tune out to a point where we barely even register it going on: a background hum on a par with the kettle. And then, quite suddenly, it becomes absolutely intolerable. The lack of creativity in their dialogue, the lack of generosity, the sheer boredom that emanates from their voices. And we snap.

So my friend snapped. On a cold, dark February evening. They were in the kitchen, which opened out, via a large glass door, onto a high-walled, rain-soaked London garden. She shoved them out there, in the pouring rain. "Go out there and fight!" she said. "Go on! Get fighting! You can come in when you've fought each other so hard you just can't fight anymore. Go on! Fight! Fight!" She locked the glass door, and the two boys—astonished by this turn of events—immediately forgot their beef with each other. They pressed their noses against the sliding glass doors and begged to be let back in.

She ignored them. Returned to her work. Every now and then, she would look up from her computer, see them tapping pathetically on the glass, and order them to start fighting again.

"You're not fighting enough. Do some fighting! Why aren't you fighting? Get on with it!"

But the boys didn't want to fight anymore. After a while— quite a while, I may add (she had a lot of work to catch up on)—she unlocked the door and let them come back in again. And they didn't exchange an angry word with each other for a week.

17. Children Unattended

There are lots of bossy laws about this. I'm not sure what they are, mind you, and don't intend to find out. I'm better off not knowing (a bit like not owning a thermometer—actual numbers will only create panic). Better to trust instinct. As it is, we all have a pretty good idea under what circumstances it feels safe to leave our children unattended: at what age, where, and for how long. Only watch out whom you tell. There are some heavyweight busybodies out there, often in places you least suspect, only waiting to get people like, well, me into trouble.

It's a wonderful thing when you first realize you can start to leave your children on their own—even if it's only to go to the store to stock up on milk. It's like a second adolescence, footloose for all of a hundred yards, if not quite fancy-free. Even so, it's hard to beat.

Leave the TV on, and the chances are the children won't even notice you're gone.

18. Police

They come to talk to our children in school, of course. Along with the nice people from the fire department, too: who send children home with a fire safety checklist for their parents. That is, my youngest daughter came home with one last week, full of fear and enthusiasm.

There's a house fire and a family burned alive about once a week in the news; although more often than not, it's a stepfather-plus-arson affair. Never mind. The girl's nervous. She wants to know why we've disabled the fire alarm. Someone, somewhere, had better track down some batteries.

It's the police who have the uphill battle when it comes to winning over our children's hearts and minds—not just in the badlands, but here and there and in the most middling of middle-class suburbs, too.

There's a law (for example) that limits the number of passengers allowed to travel in one car. It's a law that is stuck to religiously by a few, and broken on a regular basis by everyone else, because there are times—quite a lot of them—when the law is completely inconvenient. (A nursery school teacher in South Africa took it a little too far recently; she was pulled over for squeezing nineteen preschoolers into the back of her little hatchback, on an outing to a nearby playground. Bless her.)

There's another law that requires children under eight years old or under fifty-seven inches (excluding their shoes and depending on where you live) to sit on booster seats; and another, about child restraints and front seats and air bags; and almost certainly another that forbids them from traveling in the one place, mysteriously, that they most long to travel, namely in the trunk. As a result of this plethora of mini-regulations, I think many of us, when ferrying children about, do so with a vague assumption that one law or another is almost certainly being broken.

And though, to be fair to the police, I don't know of a single parent (except one on Twitter) who has been prosecuted—or even pulled over—for failing to use a booster seat, children remain only too aware that their presence in cars is subject to a mass of regulations. And even if their own parents are law-fearing, Thudguard-dependent neurotics, they will have found themselves in a car with other parents who aren't. They will have been driven in an overstuffed, underboosted car to a party somewhere, sometime. And they will be familiar with the driver's frantic cry:

Aaaarrrghh! Police! Quick! Everyone—for Christ's sake, duck!

And they tend to know the drill.

I think it's wonderful. I think it's a great leap forward for civilization that our claustrophobic, safety-obsessed, impossibly risk-averse culture has inadvertently bred a generation of children who feel comfortable waving aside the sillier, fussier points of personal safety law. You may not agree with me. It doesn't really matter. Either way, we are where we are. Our children understand that sometimes the law is an ass—and that some laws are made to be broken.

19. Punishment

Is for institutions. In family life, it seems perverse. Life is difficult enough. The idea of devising extra ways to make it even more difficult—and for the people you love most in the world—goes against common sense, against loving instinct, against human nature itself. Or certainly against mine.

In a court of law there's no love lost between the punisher and punished, and no suggestion, or even the slightest hope, that the two parties have a shared goal, let alone (to use an unfashionable phrase) that they might, in some way or another, be All in It Together. It's different for families.

Charm, luck, imagination, negotiation, good manners, and, yes, the height and color of the sky determine how we respond to one another's actions. In private family life there's something chilling about punishment (or revenge) delivered cold.

20. Drugs

Have I ever taken any, the children recently asked (before they realized how interminable and earnest my answer would be; they haven't asked again since).

What are we supposed to say? I hadn't really thought it through until the question sat there between us. Somehow, out of the mix of concern; hatred of the usual, useless humbug; perhaps even, *ahem,* enjoyment of the sound of my own voice, I came up with the following response:

Of course I have. Did I enjoy them? Well, of course I did. If drug taking wasn't enjoyable, then why would so many people go to the trouble and risk of taking them in the first place?

When they asked me which drugs, when, and why, I swear I numbed them with my windbag honesty—the highs and lows, the pros and cons of my own limited experience— and topped and tailed it all with the story of my brilliant, joyful friend, with whom I picked blackberries as a child, and built bonfires in the woods, who died of a heroin overdose, all alone, choking on her own vomit. Every mommy should have such a friend. I am grateful to her.

Who knows if children can ever really absorb the horror of it? Who knows if sharing the story with them will do any good at all? I don't suppose anything I have to say will make the slightest difference when it comes to the moment: they will be with friends, and I—and my long-dead friend—will be far from their minds. But the knowledge just might, perhaps, leave behind a small residue of caution.

Or maybe it doesn't help. I don't know. Only I know I don't want to insult their curiosity by putting them off with solemn-faced non-answers.

Also, by the way, I don't see how *any* parent can take a puritan's stance on this particular matter. If they've never tried drugs, then clearly they don't know what they're talking about and their opinions on the matter are valueless. And if they have tried them—no matter how little or how much—then they will at least understand something of the attraction. And until a parent can acknowledge that, the posture, as we say in yoga—in this case being Approach Drugs with Great Care—hasn't even begun.

21. Boundaries

Every child needs boundaries, so the wisdom goes. It's something grown-up mothers and fathers say to each other at nursery school parents' evenings, over their cocktail sausages, when they're still a little fresh to the We Are Parents protocols and they've run out of conversations about the weather. But I've always thought it sounded, at best, deluded: like a grown-up practicing its grown-upness—at worst, sinister, hinting at a dangerous penchant for absolute power.

Every Child Needs Boundaries. What does it mean, in any case? What "boundaries" are the parents referring to? Are they really suggesting, over their cocktails, that children should have their limits laid down for them in advance, and that they must be made to understand, absolutely, that these limits are nonnegotiable?

> Do not watch TV on weekdays—*but what if there's something really good on?*
> Do not answer back—*but what if there is still a point to be made?*

Do not eat sandwiches in the bath—*but, shucks, what if nobody leaves any crumbs?*

It's nonsense. It has to be. After all, there is almost nothing in the run of ordinary adult life that isn't negotiable, almost no boundary that isn't at least a little nudgeable, and the more educated people are, the more confident and successful, the richer and cleverer and more attractive they are, the better they damn well know it. Why are we so eager not to let children in on this important truth?

Aside from the fact that "boundaries" are often tiresome to uphold (and sometimes patently absurd, quite rightly rendering the "boundary enforcer" a figure of mockery and derision), boundaries serve almost no purpose—not to the child and not to the parent. Every situation is different. Every interaction is different. Every individual is different. Every conflict is annoying in a different way. No one involved is a robot. And nor, boys and girls, are mothers and fathers always right.

In fact, in any given child-parent conflict, mothers and fathers—tired, impatient, misguided, ignorant of the facts, or just too old, deaf, narrow-minded, and stupid to understand—are probably in the *wrong* no more or less often than their child is. At which point, perhaps we might be better off allowing ourselves a little room to maneuver, if only to save face. Why go to the inconvenience of lumbering ourselves with an inflexible system that insists, above all and no matter what, that we are right and our word is final, when half the time that's reasonably likely not to be the case? It's like pretending we don't fart.

Our children will find out sooner or later what nincompoops and limited people their loving parents really are. They will discover what fools and flops and flakes make up the adult world in which they must one day learn to survive. The sooner we climb down from our self-erected pedestals and treat them—and ourselves—not as predefined persons in predesignated roles, but as free and flawed individuals, *allies,* in a lonely and confusing universe, the happier and easier it might be for everyone.

I think I have only two fundamental requirements of my children (aside from the one, long since established, about saying thank you with eye contact to parents): first, that, in exchange for the roof above their heads and the chocolate cookies in the pantry; in exchange for all the emotional and financial investment, the boundless love and care, and for all the devotion and thought and unconditional support that has been put into their free and independent futures, they themselves invest in their futures, think for themselves, and embrace the world around them with energy. And second, obviously: not to be cruel.

Are those "boundaries"? Maybe they are. Beyond that, the only real boundary depends on my tolerance threshold on any given day, which, in turn, depends on the weather and the light, whether I've just been fired or been offered a pay raise, whether or not I have a hangover, and, finally, whether or not the kids have done what they've done, taken what they took, with sufficient intelligence and charm that they can somehow find a way to wriggle out of trouble. Because, of course, if they're smart about it, don't make too much noise, don't cause too much bother, and, above all, don't get caught, they can get away with pretty much anything.

Welcome to the world.

22. A Mother Is Not a Friend

A favorite assertion made by the grown-ups and the experts, in their relentless mission to quash our spontaneity and joy.

But of course a mother is a friend.

After all, what is a friend? Somebody you love and trust (and vice versa); somebody whose mistakes you forgive and whose successes you rejoice in (and vice versa); someone you respect and who respects you; who makes you laugh and makes you reconsider (and vice versa); with whom you have many things in common; who you care about and who cares about you; who you interest and who interests you; and for whom you are willing to fight.

I honestly don't know which, in the list above, isn't also to be hoped for (mutually) in a relationship between a mother and her children.

It doesn't mean you have to sit around getting high together. That would be awkward. Or, at any rate, I would find it uncomfortable. It doesn't mean all sorts of things: that your children are the best audience for a frank conversation about possible limitations and irritations of their beloved father, the agonizing pointlessness of existence, or the fact that you or he or both have just taken a lover. But of course it's a friendship! My children are my friends. Most certainly. And I am their friend—their close and loyal friend—and I sincerely hope I always will be.

23. Boredom

When I was a child, it was a major ingredient of every weekend and school holiday. So much so, I invented a song. I would lie on my bed with my feet resting against the wall and sing it on a single note, for surprisingly long stretches:

Bor-ing
Bor-ing
What shall we do?
Typhoo
Boring

It killed hours—days probably, if you totaled them up. Eventually the sheer b-o-r-e-d-o-m of the song would drive me, half zombified, to do something else. And, in desultory fashion, I would find another way to not-quite-amuse myself, until the next option presented itself. Boredom, as much as necessity, was ever the mother of invention. Not everything invented has to be worthwhile.

Boredom is part of childhood. Actually, it's part of life.

Learning to cope with it is one of the great requirements of adulthood. So it's a mystery why we modern parents go to such neurotic lengths to banish it from our children's lives.

Sometimes just sitting and thinking is good.

24. The Epiphany

There are a couple of tennis courts quite near our house, which the children are allowed to play on. At the far end of one of them there is also a wall, which means that if they can't find another human to play tennis with, they can always play against that. One of my fellow school mothers—clever and likable in all respects, guilty about having to work through her children's holidays, neurotic about her child spending any time not sensibly designated—e-mailed me that she had found a tennis coach. She had two other children lined up to share the lesson, and she wondered if my child wanted to be the fourth. The cost could then be divided among the four children. She said she had haggled the price down, and I'm sure she had. Nevertheless, it still cost money that, not only did I not want to spend on tennis coaching, I didn't want to have to remember to have in my wallet, to hand to my child to hand to the coach on the right morning of the right day each week. For a tennis lesson that, frankly, my child could easily do without.

I ignored the e-mail (often a fail-safe response) and several other e-mails that followed. But then, as luck would have it, I bumped into her in person.

She said: "Oooh, I've been wanting to talk to you," and she presented her case. To which I replied:

"I can't really afford it."

This statement can embarrass people, especially if they are noticeably richer than you are, which renders it doubly effective. In general it's an excellent line to drop, if you're not brave enough to say,

"It's just that I'd prefer to spend the cash on something else."

or

"Hmm. It all sounds a bit of a hassle."

(Both of which, in this instance, would have been closer to the truth.)

She was quite embarrassed. Because she is a nice woman. And because she is noticeably richer than I am. She said: But if we divide the cost by four . . . And if we pay for five or ten lessons in advance . . .

To which I replied: "In any case, there's a court there for them. Why can't they just hit against each other?"

She looked taken aback. I don't think the possibility had even occurred to her. "They'd only mess around . . . ," she said.

"Not if they want to play, they won't mess around," I replied. "And if they *don't* want to play, so what? I don't care if they mess around. As long as I'm not paying for it. Do you?"

If I'd been speaking Japanese, she might have understood me better. She wandered away looking slightly shell-shocked, and I wondered if I had been rude.

It was the end of the discussion. And the beginning of a new extracurricular-free life. It so happens, at the end of a long and boring day, that my children can often be found hitting a tennis ball listlessly against that tennis court wall. Or not. Sometimes they're lolling against the wall, chatting. Or lying on the tarmac, staring at the clouds. Or lying on the tarmac, squabbling.

It doesn't cost a thing. It's another way of passing the time. Or, at least, another location to pass it in. And it's within walking distance of home.

25. The Magic of Childhood

We adults harp on about the magic of childhood as if we'd stumbled on a new religion. But a part of the magic (which often drives parents to distraction) is the childish lack of hurry—the liberated sense that to waste an hour staring at the clouds matters not a wit because there are *infinite* hours where that one came from.

Children have all the time in the world. Lucky things. So what if they spend vast tracts of it simply gestating? Previously known as "relaxing." I only wish I could learn from them and remember how to do it half so well myself.

Computer games are a waste of time. We know that. Lying on the sofa staring at the ceiling is a waste of time. Spending all morning in bed . . . watching *Harry Potter and the Order of the Phoenix* for the 30,987th time . . . In due course children will grow out of their inertia—and they will start racing around with fraught, gray scowls on their faces, dividing their days into dismal little units of to-do, just like their parents. In the meantime, let us save ourselves the money, the gas, the time and energy, the guilt, the sheer boredom of having to organize alternatives, and leave them in peace to do what they really want to do: as often as not, absolutely nothing at all.

Also, by the way, there's something a bit pathetic about children who need to be spoon-fed adult-approved amusement every moment of the day. Isn't there? It's a bit feeble, isn't it? Don't they have any resources of their own, for God's sake? No spirit of adventure? No desire for privacy or independence or rebellion? *Anything?*

The magic of childhood. Those four words together conjure up something golden: perhaps an ad just before Christmas. Supermarkets always love a Magic of Childhood Christmas theme. There's handsome Dad driving through the snow, and a smiling wife and a real log fire and an amazingly well-decorated tree—and there'll be food enough to feed the five thousand, laid out and glistening on platters, and a couple of bouncing, shiny children in clean pajamas, and lots and lots of symmetrically wrapped presents.

The Magic of Childhood! Presents are certainly part of it (no arguing with that). As indeed are Christmas trees and happy homes and clean pajamas. And that sense of absolute security—which those ads portray so well, and which children can feel sometimes, in the bosom of their family.

Sadly, in our desperation to capture, style, package, share, and, above all, render *safe* the magic we all remember so fondly, I think we sometimes end up doing the opposite. We spend fortunes, we bend over backward, we fly our children to Disneyland, and take family breaks to Lapland (words fail me). So much adult interference, so much purpose-specific equipment, so much preplanning and presanitizing perfection, which makes it all the harder to be lost in an experience. With all our goodwill and open wallets, I wonder if we don't succeed only in sucking the magic out of everything.

Certainly, I know that all my most magical, happiest childhood memories (aside from the opening of presents, obviously) involved adventures—voyages of danger and discovery—not with adults and their interminable "don't"s and "be careful"s tagging needlessly along, but with other children, as wide-eyed, excited, and fearful as I was.

The real magic of childhood is an open, childlike mind and a free spirit, both of which are better accessed when the adults butt out, find their own amusements, and leave the children in peace to enjoy their childlike fun alone.

Christmas Eve

As I write these last few words, I realize there's a faint danger, on their publication, that the social workers may come knocking, and the police, and the midwives, too; and the child psychologists, the road safety experts, and the super-moms and the health visitors, and the doctors and the sports teachers, and the makers of television commercials, and the soppy dads and the stay-at-home moms. In fact, just thinking about all the people who might want to come knocking makes me want to retire to my room for a good long nap, and wake up only when they promise they've found something else to disapprove of.

The fact is, I wouldn't have dared to write this when the children were still babies, for fear of all the things we all fear: all the things that might go wrong. But they didn't go wrong; despite all the shortcuts, the wanton selfishness of this loving mom, here I am with two children almost grown and a third with her babyhood far behind her. Three healthy children who, despite their shamelessly mediocre mother, are doing just fine. Or better than fine, actually. Much better than fine, if you ask me. But then again, I am their mother.

As I tap out these final words, all three of them are within eyeshot.

My oldest daughter, fifteen, is stretched out on a sofa in the far corner, teeth covered in Super Glue, she says, having tried and failed to fix her orthodontic brace. (There's no way around it: I suppose we will have to make an appointment.) She is watching a DVD of the French movie *Subway*, in search of the exact quote you will have read, on page 129. The task defeated me (the film hasn't aged well), so I've bribed her to watch it for me. I thought five dollars was more than generous, with tea and a cookie thrown in. But she must have smelled my desperation, because somehow she's haggled me up to an astronomical ten dollars.

My son, twelve, is playing "keepie-uppie" right here beside me—beside my laptop, more to the point (it's making me nervous)—and talking to me as I write. He's talking ludicrously fast. *Bounce-bounce . . .* Saying something about a *one-touch dummy run . . .* something . . . *back-heeling a corner kick to the far post . . .* and a referee . . . and God only knows if he's talking about a game he actually played or something that happened between Chelsea and—Sunderland? It doesn't matter. He knows I'm not listening. It's part of his personal joke. He's killing time until Christmas begins, demonstrating his freakish ability to say very, very dull things very, very quickly (while playing keepie-uppie), until the sheer idiocy—and the volume—threatens to kill me with boredom and I beg him to stop. I'm laughing as I write this, but in a moment, we both know, I will break.

The six-year-old is in the hallway, her father's laptop on the floor in front of her, teaching herself the dance steps to a new Olly Murs video she's found on YouTube. There's a lot of hip jiving going on; outrageous levels of hip jiving, in fact. I've just told her she was dancing like a slapper. It's hard to tell if she knows what a slapper is. But I think she got the gist. She laughed like a drain and hip jived even harder.

My magical children. Or magical to me, at any rate. Funny. Resourceful. Excellent company. And happy, I think. For the moment, anyway. I am more proud of them than it is possible to say.

I must admit I am not entirely certain where their magical father may be. It's the party season, after all. If he told me where he was going, I probably wasn't listening. Tonight, in any case, at some point soon, we'll all be back sharing the same house again. We shall be hanging our magical children's ridiculous Christmas stockings, the contents of which, fresh from the cheap stores of Hammersmith, are lying in a scrappy heap on our bedroom floor, awaiting our soon-to-be-drunken attention.

Yes, the sun could be shining. We could be in the Caribbean. We might have won the lottery. My daughter's teeth might not be covered in Super Glue, our heads might be nit-free zones, I might have sworn a little less, my workaholic husband might have been around a little more, the central heating might be working. But aside from that, we seem to be in reasonable shape. There are no martyrs among us and no victims. Just five individuals, hungry for life, who love each other, enjoy each other's company, and are very much looking forward to Christmas. Tomorrow the cousinly hordes will gather. But tonight it's just us. And Chinese takeout. Who knows what lies ahead? But as we each live this moment, I don't believe family life could be any better.

They fuck you up, your mum and dad. One way or another, no matter what we do or don't do, I dare say we always will. But with a little less fretting and hassling, we might at least have a better time of it in the process.

Index

About the Author

Daisy Waugh has written on family for the British *Independent*, the *Daily Telegraph*, and in a weekly humor column for *The Sunday Times*. She has also been a presenter on BBC radio and Channel 4 television and has written six novels. She lives in London with her husband and three children.